# modern
# mezze

# modern mezze

## anissa helou

photographs by Vanessa Courtier

Quadrille

## notes

- All spoon measures are level unless otherwise stated: 1 tsp = 5ml spoon; 1 tbsp = 15ml spoon.
- Fresh herbs are used, unless dried herbs are specified in a recipe.
- I recommend that you use medium organic or free-range eggs, as I do. Anyone who is pregnant or in a vulnerable health group should avoid recipes using raw or lightly cooked eggs.
- Use good quality sea salt and freshly ground black pepper.
- Timings are for conventional ovens. If using a fan-assisted oven, reduce the temperature by 10–15°C (1/2 Gas mark) and check the dish towards the end of cooking as it may be ready a little sooner. Use an oven thermometer to check the accuracy of your oven settings.

# introduction

'Leisurely savouring a tremendous selection of small dishes' is probably the most appropriate way to define mezze. For many years, this style of eating has been somewhat of a secret in the west, known to, and enjoyed almost exclusively by, the 'foodie' elite, most notably among them Elisabeth David. However, today's trend for informal, unstructured, yet healthy meals has finally propelled this Levantine way of eating into the mainstream and has made mezze the order of the day.

But for me, mezze were the order of the day from when I was born... well almost. Whenever my father came back from a long business trip, we would celebrate by going to one of the riverside mezze restaurants in Zahleh, a town north east of Beirut.

Our excitement at these outings started building up from the day before and lasted long after we returned home. First, there was my father's huge Buick, which we loved climbing into. Then there was the bridge to the restaurant, which was lined with street vendors peddling all kinds of nuts and sweets, though we had to wait until the journey back to buy anything. And once we had settled at the large table overlooking the river, we became even more animated as we listened to the waiter describing the mezzes on offer, butting in every now and then to request our favourites.

My father never looked at the menu. Instead he would ask the waiter to tell him what was good on that day, referring not to mezze staples such as hommus, tabbûlé or *baba ghannûge*, but rather to what was in season or to what needed to be supremely fresh. Did they have *sliq*, a generic term used to describe all kinds of wild greens sautéed in olive oil and garnished with caramelised onions? Or did they have *'asafeer*, the tiniest and most succulent birds that would be frowned upon here? And how fresh was the raw meat?

The questions would continue until my father had ordered as many as twenty different mezzes. Throughout the whole exchange, we would crack open roasted pumpkin seeds, which the waiter had brought us, along with crudités, olives and nuts to nibble on while waiting for our order.

Our excitement reached a new peak when the food started arriving. The waiters brought tray after tray of small dishes, all cleverly stacked so that the food stayed intact inside. The dishes were gorgeously garnished – the raw meats with fresh herbs, the dips with sprinklings of brightly coloured spices or pomegranate seeds, the salads with tiny cubes of shiny red tomatoes, the savoury pastries with bright yellow lemon wedges, and so on. The feast was as much for the eye as for the appetite.

We ate straight from the serving dishes, scooping our food with torn pieces of pita bread, trying to keep our fingers clean. As soon as one dish was finished, the waiter would quickly remove it and replace it with another. And whenever we got bored, we left our parents to their conversation and went to play by the water. My parents didn't mind. It is accepted practice for people to come and go from a mezze table. Nor did they worry about us children coming to any harm. The waiters kept a watchful eye over us. In Lebanon, as in other Mediterranean countries like Italy, children are always welcomed and everyone feels protective towards them.

When we'd had enough of playing and started feeling peckish again, we would return to find new dishes added to the spread. The pleasure of the meal seemed to last forever.

However, this endless mezze is really the preserve of restaurant eating, not only in Lebanon but also in other countries with a mezze tradition: Syria, Jordan, Egypt, Turkey, Greece and the Balkans, all once occupied by the Ottomans. It would take too long or you would need more than one cook to prepare such a huge spread at home. This is not to say that people don't serve mezze at home. Quite the opposite. It's just that the home-style spread is different – with fewer dishes, served in larger quantities.

# mezze at home

The word mezze comes from the Persian verb *maza* – meaning to taste, to relish. And the most important thing to remember when you are serving a mezze at home is to make sure that the flavours of the different dishes are harmonious, while the colours and textures on the table are contrasting.

I often serve a mezze when friends or family visit. I usually prepare three or four dishes: a dip, a salad or two, a vegetable dish and, if time, some savoury pastries. To enhance the spread, I rely on our tradition of *zinet al-tawleh* (decoration of the table). This is an assortment of bread, crudités, olives and pickles laid on the table to make it look plentiful and to give diners something to nibble on while waiting for other food to be served. It's a brilliant way of expanding the spread without spending any extra time in the kitchen, and I suggest you do the same. Here are some ideas:

**Crudités** add colour and crunch to your mezze table. Serve carrots and cucumbers, quartered lengthways, lightly salted and sprinkled with lemon juice. Or radishes, pre-soaked in cold water for a couple of hours to sweeten and crisp them up. Or simply offer a bowl of cherry tomatoes (vine-ripened and organic as they taste better).

**Olives** are another essential inclusion and, again, you will find a wonderful selection of olives in most Middle Eastern shops. (For further information, see page 49.)

As for **roasted nuts** and **seeds**, you can serve them either salted or flavoured with lemon juice. You can also **roast chickpeas**, one of my favourite childhood snacks. Simply toss ready-cooked chickpeas in a little olive oil, spread them on a baking sheet and roast in a moderate oven at 180°C/Gas 4 for about 1 hour until crisp. *Illustrated above*

If you feel like being extravagant, buy some **bottarga** – dried mullet's roe, called *batrakh* in Arabic and *avgotaracho* in Greek. Serve it thinly sliced, drizzled with olive oil and topped with slivers of garlic.

And when **sea urchins** are in season, add these to your spread. They make a splendid mezze. When I lived in Lebanon, I often had a huge platter of sea urchins on the beach for lunch – collected off the rocks by young boys who then sold them to the beach restaurant.

**Cheese** is another excellent, quick mezze. Serve cubed feta, drizzled with a little good olive oil and sprinkled with Aleppo pepper. Alternatively, serve thinly sliced kashkaval (a kind of eastern Mediterranean Manchego), known as *qashqawan* in Arabic.

**Labné** balls preserved in olive oil are also a delicious mezze and you can buy them from most Middle Eastern food shops. I particularly like to serve them sprinkled with a little dried chilli. *Illustrated above*

**Pickles** are a must at a mezze table. You can, of course, make your own but you can also buy excellent commercial pickles from Middle Eastern shops. (For more information, see page 145.)

Another great addition to your mezze spread is thinly sliced **pasturma**, a kind of spicy Turkish/Armenian bresaola and the only cured meat in the Middle East. *Illustrated right*

# drinks to serve with mezze

The choice of drinks to serve with mezze is between alcoholic and soft drinks, depending on your inclination or religious belief. The traditional alcoholic choice is arak (ouzo in Greek and raki in Turkish), a clear liquor made by distilling grape juice and flavouring it with anise. Arak is aged in earthenware jars for 1–2 years but unlike wine, it does not improve with longer ageing. After 4 to 5 years, it turns yellow and loses much of its taste.

Arak is too strong to drink on its own and needs to be mixed with water. It is always served in small tumblers and the ratio is usually one-third arak to two-thirds water. You can increase it to 50/50 but the drink will be very strong. The way to serve arak is to pour it first, then add the water and finally the ice cubes. As you add the water, you will notice the alcohol immediately turning a cloudy white. *Illustrated right*

Arak may be the traditional choice, but it is not the only one. There are many good local wines, mainly from Lebanon and Greece, that go with mezze. My favourite is the Lebanese Musar, and not only the world-famous red Château Musar. Cuvée Musar and Serge Hochar are both cheaper and less complex, and in a way better suited to the multiple flavours of mezze. Musar also make an unusual rosé, more of a cross between a light red and a rosé, which is ideal in the summer. And of course, there are many excellent light local beers to choose from.

As for soft drinks, the choice is far from dull. You can serve fresh pomegranate juice, making it even more intriguing by adding a pinch of cinnamon and a few drops of orange blossom water. Or fresh lemonade, adding a little zest to give it a hint of bitterness. Or a delightfully refreshing almond milk. The 'milk' is made by pulverising soaked blanched almonds with a little sugar, letting the paste steep in water, then straining it. Adding a little orange blossom water will make the drink even more exotic.

In Morocco, they even make water taste exotic. A few grains of mastic (a resin collected off the *Pistacia lentiscus* tree) are thrown on to a small charcoal fire over which an earthenware jar is inverted. By the time the grains finish burning, the inside of the jar is infused with the fragrance of mastic. It is then filled with water, covered and placed in a cool place. Sometimes a few drops of orange blossom water are added. I never imagined that water could be a heady drink, but in this case it is!

# the mezze larder

Before you can prepare and serve mezze, you need to stock up on a few key ingredients. Fortunately, with the trend for global cooking, most of these are readily available, if not in supermarkets, then certainly in Middle Eastern shops. Most ingredients have a long shelf life and once they are in your storecupboard, all you will need to do in order to prepare a wonderful mezze spread is to shop for fresh ingredients.

**Pulses** are essential for most mezze spreads. You can buy them dried or you can shorten your preparation time by buying them pre-cooked. In Spanish markets, there are special stalls where you can buy freshly cooked pulses but here you have to rely on those that are preserved in glass jars. The best come from France, Italy or Spain.

**Burghul** is something else you need to keep in your larder – both fine and coarse varieties. The quality and texture of the burghul sold in Middle Eastern shops is by far superior to any you will find in a health shop or supermarkets. In Turkish shops, the grain will be very light in colour, while in Lebanese shops it will be dark. The difference in colour is due to the different wheat used. I also suggest you stock up on frikeh – green, roasted cracked wheat with a superb, unmistakable smoky flavour.
*Illustrated right (rinsed, fine burghul)*

**Pomegranate syrup** gives a subtle sweet-savoury flavour to fried vegetables and other dishes. The syrup is made by boiling down the juice of sour pomegranates until reduced to a thick, dark brown liquid.

**Tahini** is another important ingredient in the mezze larder. It is a creamy, oily paste, which is extracted from sesame seeds. Tahini is used in dips and dressings, and also sauces. Here I suggest you buy an Arab brand of tahini, which will be lighter and smoother than most others. You may also want to keep a small stock of sesame seeds, which you can buy ready-toasted, to use as garnish.

walnuts, pistachios and hazelnuts. Nuts deteriorate relatively quickly, so buy little and often. They will also keep better in the fridge or freezer than in a kitchen cupboard.

**Dried mint** and **vine leaves** are also essential ingredients. You can buy excellent vine leaves preserved in brine, or vacuum packed. And if you have any growing in your garden, pick them at the right time of the year (early in the season), blanch and freeze them. They freeze extremely well and have the advantage of not being salty, in the way that preserved vine leaves are.

And finally you mustn't forget to keep a good stock of **extra virgin olive oil**. A light one for cooking and the best you can afford to use in salads and to drizzle over dips.

In the fridge, it is a good idea to keep **lemons**, **garlic**, **onions** and **fresh herbs**. Store the herbs in sealed plastic bags in the salad drawer and turn the bags over every couple of days to shift the condensation. This will preserve the herbs for a few days longer.

**Sumac** is a lemony flavouring, ground from the dried berries of the *Rhus coriaria*. It is used to flavour salads, fried eggs and grilled meats. Sumac is also gorgeous sprinkled over some dips. *Illustrated above*

**Za'tar** is another important mezze ingredient. This mixture of dried thyme, sumac and sesame seeds is available in different styles: the brown Syrian mix, the green Jordanian mix and Lebanese za'tar, which is greyish in colour. All are good and can be interchanged in recipes calling for za'tar.

**Spices** feature in many mezze dishes, notably cumin, cinnamon, paprika, cayenne, Aleppo pepper, Lebanese 7-spice mixture and allspice. For the best flavour, buy spices in small amounts and restock regularly. Ground spices are best stored in hermetically sealed containers in a cool, dark kitchen cupboard.

**Nuts** are another mezze staple. You'll need pine nuts (preferably the Mediterranean type),

# menus

The following suggestions are divided into menus for serving mezze as a starter, and menus for mezze as a meal. Each serves 4 to 6. If you want to serve a larger number, simply double the quantities suggested in the recipes; or add more dishes if you have time. If you are serving mezze as a starter, I suggest you follow with a simple main course such as a roast or a tagine. Bread is a must at the mezze table, as are crudités, olives and pickles, and, of course, you can add ready-made delicacies (see pages 9–10).

**Mezze as a Starter**

Dried Broad Bean Dip
(page 32)
Aubergine Bites (page 66)
Purslane, Tomato and Cucumber
Salad (page 63)
Crudités, Olives, Bread, Pickles

—

Peanut and Chickpea Dry Dip
(page 37)
Fried Okra (page 96)
Spicy Cheese Filo Parcels
(page 72)
Crudités, Olives, Bread, Pickles

—

Za'tar Bites (page 66)
Pine Nut Tarator (page 36)
Courgettes in Tomato Sauce
(page 109)
Crudités, Olives, Bread, Pickles

—

Tahini Dip (page 28)
Falafel (page 88)
Wild Chicory in Olive Oil
(page 103)
Crudités, Olives, Bread, Pickles

Grilled Aubergine Dip
(page 29)
Cabbage Salad (page 58)
Tomato Burgers
(page 114)
Crudités, Olives, Bread, Pickles

—

Taramasalata (page 33)
Fried Aubergines (page 108)
Green Beans in Tomato Sauce
(page 102)
Crudités, Olives, Bread, Pickles

—

Walnut Tarator (page 36)
Turkish Mussel Brochettes
(page 120)
Rocket with Tomatoes
(page 42)
Crudités, Olives, Bread, Pickles

—

Chilli and Herb Dip (page 22)
Sardines Chermûla
(page 130)
Rice Tabbûlé (page 46)
Crudités, Olives, Bread, Pickles

Barbecued Chicken Wings
(page 136)
Labné Filo Parcels (page 72)
Thyme and Rocket Salad
(page 42)
Crudités, Olives, Bread, Pickles

—

Sautéed Chicken Livers
(page 139)
Lentils in Olive Oil (page 86)
Herb and Toasted Pita Salad
(page 60)
Crudités, Olives, Bread, Pickles

—

Nayla's Herb Kibbé
(page 151)
Spinach Filo Parcels
(page 72)
Grilled Pepper Salad (page 59)
Crudités, Olives, Bread, Pickles

—

Hommus (page 21)
Quail's Eggs with Spicy Sausage
(page 152)
White Tabbûlé (page 46)
Crudités, Olives, Bread, Pickles

## Mezze as a Meal

Tzatziki (page 27)
Burghul and Nut Burgers
(page 90)
Grilled Aubergine Salad (page 52)
Za'tar Bites (page 66)
Wild Chicory in Olive Oil (page
103)
Crudités, Olives, Bread, Pickles

—

Labné and Thyme Dip
(page 27)
Moroccan Carrot Salad (page 54)
Turkish Grilled Peppers (page 104)
Giant Bean Salad (page 92)
Purslane, Tomato and Cucumber
Salad (page 63)
Crudités, Olives, Bread, Pickles

—

Grilled Aubergine Dip (page 29)
Spinach Filo Parcels (page 72)
Sardines wrapped in Vine Leaves
(page 127)
Smoked Wheat 'Risotto' (page 87)
Cabbage Salad (page 58)
Crudités, Olives, Bread, Pickles

—

Mackerel and Hazelnut Dip
(page 37)
Fried Whitebait (or baby octopus)
(page 124)
Grilled Pepper Salad (page 59)
Broad Bean 'Risotto' (page 84)
Crudités, Olives, Bread, Pickles

Turkish Mussel 'Risotto'
(page 125)
Cheese and Cucumber Wrap
(page 79)
Pine Nut Tarator (page 36)
Fried Whitebait (page 124)
Moroccan Stuffed Tomatoes
(page 98)
Crudités, Olives, Bread, Pickles

—

Lebanese Tomato Salsa (page 30)
Grilled Spiced Quail (page 141)
Carrots and Lentils (page 83)
Thyme and Rocket Salad (page 42)
Feta Cheese Salad (page 50)
Crudités, Olives, Bread, Pickles

—

Hommus (page 21)
Courgettes in Tomato Sauce
(page 109)
Barbecued Chicken Wings
(page 136)
Herb and Toasted Pita Salad
(page 60)
Lebanese Potato and Basil Wrap
(page 78)
Crudités, Olives, Bread, Pickles

—

Tabbûlé (page 45)
Spiced Herby Meat Balls
(page 143)
Spicy Fried Potatoes (page 116)
Lebanese Bruschetta (page 69)
Green Beans in Tomato Sauce
(page 102)
Crudités, Olives, Bread, Pickles

Cheese and Pepper Dip
(page 28)
Turkish Burghul Salad
(page 47)
Spicy Lamb Bites (page 66)
Stuffed Aubergines (page 112)
Rocket with Tomatoes
(page 42)
Crudités, Olives, Bread, Pickles

—

Harissa (page 38)
Moroccan Spiced Herby Meat
Balls (page 143)
Greek Giant Baked Beans
(page 91)
Herb and Toasted Pita Salad
(page 60)
Crudités, Olives, Bread, Pickles

—

Fried Cauliflower (page 111)
Stuffed Vine Leaves
(page 115)
Turkish Kibbé (page 150)
Purslane, Tomato and Cucumber
Salad (page 63)
Crudités, Olives, Bread, Pickles

—

Kibbé Balls (page 146)
Tzatziki flavoured with mint
(page 27)
Cabbage Salad (page 58)
Moroccan Aubergine Salad
(page 53)
Crudités, Olives, Bread, Pickles

# hommus, tzatziki and other dips

# hommus

*hommûs*

**serves 4**
660g jar chickpeas (425g net weight)
100ml tahini
juice of 1½ lemons, or to taste
1 garlic clove, peeled and crushed
fine sea salt

*for the garnish*
sweet paprika
extra virgin olive oil
1 tbsp chopped flat-leaf parsley (optional)

I used to make hommus the old-fashioned slow way, using dried chickpeas, mainly because I'm not keen on the taste of canned chickpeas. However, you can now buy jars of excellent ready-cooked chickpeas, preserved in water and salt, without added artificial preservatives. The best come from France, Italy and Spain. Just be sure to rinse them well before using, to get rid of excess salt.

Drain the chickpeas, rinse well and drain thoroughly. Put them in a food processor with the tahini and lemon juice and process until very smooth. Transfer to a bowl.

Add the garlic and salt to taste, mixing well. If the hommus is too thick, add a little more lemon juice, or water if the flavour is already tart enough. Taste and adjust the seasoning.

Spoon the hommus into a shallow serving dish. With the back of the spoon, spread it across the dish, raising it slightly at the edges and in the centre, so that you have a shallow groove in between. Sprinkle a little paprika over the raised edges and drizzle a little olive oil in the groove. Sprinkle the parsley in the centre, if using. Serve with pita or *marqûq* bread.

# chilli and herb dip

*————————z'hûg*

**serves 4–6**
250g fresh red chilli
  peppers, trimmed
5 garlic cloves, peeled
100g coriander sprigs,
  most of the stalk removed
100g flat-leaf parsley, most
  of the stalk removed
1 tsp ground cumin
pinch of ground cardamom
1 tsp sea salt
1 tsp freshly ground black
  pepper
2 tbsp extra virgin olive oil

This is the Israeli/Yemini equivalent of Tunisian harissa. It is either used as a dip with bread, or as a spread in place of butter in sandwiches. You can use green chillies if you like, but make it a mixture of mild and hot ones, so that the dip is not too fiery.

Halve and deseed the chillies, cut them into chunks and place in a food processor with the garlic. Whiz to chop coarsely. Add the herbs, spices, seasoning and olive oil and continue processing until you have a lightly textured paste.

Serve immediately, or transfer the dip to a jar with a tight-fitting lid and refrigerate. It will keep for up to a week in the fridge.

# pita &
# other breads

Mezze is all about sharing food and eating it straight from serving dishes. And rather than use forks to pick up food, diners generally tear pieces of bread and use these to scoop up food from the dishes.

In Lebanon, Syria, Greece and Egypt pita is the bread to serve with mezze. Arab pita is a large round bread that separates into two very thin, equal layers. Whether it is made in large modern or small primitive bakeries, the process is more or less the same and almost fully automated.

The dough is kneaded and cut into pieces by machine, then fed through rollers, which flatten the pieces into perfect discs. After proving, they are transferred to a very hot oven where they puff up and bake within seconds. The pitas deflate as they cool and are then ready for packing, or to be sold directly from the bakery.

Pita is known as *khobz arabi* (Arabic bread) in Lebanon; *aysh baladi* (local bread) in Egypt; and *khobz shami* (Damascene bread) in Syria. Pita is the name used in Greece, Cyprus and Israel, and of course in the west, where the bread is smaller, thicker and often oval. Greek pita is the only pita to have no pocket.

Pita is often toasted. I like to split it into two discs and cut these into triangles, the size of corn chips. I then spread the triangles on a baking sheet and bake them in a moderate oven at 180°C/Gas 4 for a few minutes until golden brown. These pita chips (see left) are great served with dips.

Despite the name, Turkish *pide* is quite different from either Arab or Greek pita. It has a soft crumb and crust, more like a thick focaccia, but shaped long and oval, and often topped with sesame seeds.

There is also a whole family of ultra thin, one-layered breads such as *marqûq, knobz tannûr, lavash, yufka* and *gözleme*, which are all very large and very thin, and variations on the same theme. They are usually cooked on a *saj*, which looks like a huge inverted wok in Lebanon, though it is flat in Turkey. The exception is *khobz tannûr*, which as the name indicates is baked in a *tannûr*, a kind of pit oven above ground – possibly the earliest oven in history.

However, you do not have to limit yourself to serving Arab, Greek or Turkish bread with your mezze. You can offer other Mediterranean breads, such as the Sardinian *pane carasau*, which is more commonly, if wrongly, known as *carta da musica* – a thin cracker that is perfect with dips. Ciabatta, focaccia, fougasse and grissini (Italian breadsticks) are also great to serve on a mezze table.

# tzatziki

*cacik/laban ma' khiyar*

This dip is found with slight variations in Turkey, Greece, Lebanon and Syria. The following recipe is Turkish in origin. For a Lebanese or Syrian version, replace the dill with 1–2 tbsp powdered dried mint.

If using small cucumbers, halve lengthways and slice thinly. If you have a standard cucumber, peel, halve, deseed and grate, then salt lightly. Let sit for about 15 minutes, then squeeze to get rid of excess moisture.

Mix the cucumber, yoghurt, garlic and dill together in a bowl. Taste and adjust the salt if necessary. Spoon into a serving dish, drizzle with a little olive oil and sprinkle with a little paprika. Serve garnished with dill.

**serves 4**
4 small Middle Eastern or
   1 regular cucumber(s)
sea salt
450g Greek style yoghurt
1 garlic clove, peeled and
   crushed
2–3 tbsp chopped dill

*for the garnish*
extra virgin olive oil
paprika, for sprinkling
dill sprigs

# labné and thyme dip

*labneh bil-za'tar* ───────

It will take you less than 5 minutes to produce this delectable dip with ready-made labné. However, I prefer to make my own, by gathering goat's milk yoghurt in muslin to form a pouch and hanging it over the sink to drain off excess liquid overnight. You can also use cow's or sheep's milk yoghurt.

**serves 4**
300g labné (see left)
3 tbsp za'tar
3 tbsp extra virgin olive oil, plus extra for garnish
fine sea salt
toasted sesame seeds, for garnish

Mix the labné, za'tar and olive oil together in a bowl. Taste and add salt if necessary – some za'tar mixes can be very salty.

Spoon the dip into a serving bowl, making grooves here and there. Drizzle a little olive oil in the grooves. Sprinkle the surface lightly with toasted sesame seeds and serve with crudités.

# tahini dip
*———— tarator*

A delicious, addictive dip, which becomes a salad dressing if you dilute it with a little more water or lemon juice. To liven it up, add 3 tbsp finely chopped parsley or coriander if you like. And if you are really not keen on garlic, simply leave it out.

**serves 4**
150ml tahini
juice of 1½ lemons, or to taste
1 garlic clove, peeled and crushed
sea salt

Put the tahini in a bowl and gradually stir in the lemon juice, alternately with 100ml water. It will first thicken, then become thinner as you add more liquid. Taste the dip before you add all the lemon juice – if you use less, make up the difference with water. Keep stirring until it is the consistency of double cream. Add the garlic and salt to taste and mix well. Serve with crudités, pita chips (page 25) or fried cauliflower (page 111).

# cheese and pepper dip
*———— çokelekli biber kavurması*

A combination of feta and curd cheese makes a good substitute for *çokelek* – the authentic curd cheese for this dip, which you are unlikely to find in the west. Alternatively, you can make your own by boiling yoghurt with a little lemon juice until it curdles, then straining it through muslin.

**serves 4–6**
4 tbsp extra virgin olive oil
1 green pepper, trimmed, deseeded and diced
200g feta cheese, crumbled
225g curd cheese
¾ tsp Turkish pepper

Heat the olive oil in a large frying pan over a medium heat and fry the green pepper, stirring occasionally, until soft. Add the cheeses and the Turkish pepper and stir for 2–3 minutes, or until the cheeses are well combined and have melted. Transfer to a serving bowl and serve warm, or at room temperature.

# grilled
## aubergine dip
### *baba ghannûge* ————

**serves 4**
6 large aubergines, about
 250g each
4 tbsp tahini
sea salt
juice of 1 lemon, or to taste
1 garlic clove, peeled and
 crushed

*for the garnish*
extra virgin olive oil
1 tbsp chopped mint or
 fresh pomegranate seeds
 (ideally the sour type)

There is some confusion over the Arabic name of this dip. In Syria, it is *mûtabbal*, while *baba ghannûge* is used to describe a grilled aubergine salad (page 52). In any case it is exceptionally good, provided the aubergines are char-grilled or, better still, barbecued over an open fire so they take on a smoky flavour. It is also important to mash the aubergines by hand – if you use a food processor the dip won't have such a good texture.

Preheat the grill to high. Prick the aubergines in several places with a small knife (to stop them bursting under the grill) and place on a sturdy baking sheet or grill rack. Grill until the aubergines are very soft to the touch and the skins are slightly charred, turning to expose all sides evenly to the heat. (Or cook on a barbecue.) This may take up to 45 minutes, depending on the heat.

Transfer the aubergines to a board, halve each one lengthways and scoop out the flesh with a spoon. Put the flesh into a colander and leave for at least half an hour to drain off the excess liquid.

Tip the aubergine flesh into a wide bowl and mash, using a potato masher or the back of a fork. Don't crush it too much – you want the dip to have texture. Add the tahini and salt to taste and mix well, then stir in the lemon juice and crushed garlic. Taste and adjust the seasoning if necessary.

Transfer the dip to a shallow serving bowl and with the back of a spoon, spread it the same way as you would hommus (page 21) so that you have a shallow groove in the dip. Drizzle a little olive oil in the groove and sprinkle the mint or pomegranate seeds decoratively in the centre and at regular intervals along the raised edge. Serve with pita bread.

# lebanese
# **tomato** salsa
— *banadûrah harrah*

An unusual dip that needs to be used sparingly as it is rather spicy. It is delicious on its own with pita bread, pita chips (page 25), or even slices of baguette. It also goes well with fried aubergines (page 108), grilled spiced quail (page 141) and spiced herby meat balls (page 143).

Peel, deseed and finely dice the tomatoes. Heat the olive oil in a pan over a medium heat. When it is hot, add the tomatoes and garlic and cook, stirring regularly, for 5 minutes.

Add the cayenne pepper and dried mint. Season with salt to taste and cook for another 5 minutes, stirring regularly. By now, the tomatoes should have lost all their excess liquid. Taste and adjust the seasoning if necessary. Set aside to cool.

Serve the tomato salsa at room temperature.

**note**  To peel the tomatoes, cut out the stalks, then place in a bowl and pour boiling water over them to loosen the skins. Remove and peel away the skins.

**serves 4–6**
1kg firm, ripe tomatoes
3 tbsp extra virgin olive oil
3 garlic cloves, peeled and crushed
1 tsp cayenne pepper
1 tbsp dried mint
sea salt

# dried **broad bean** dip

*—————— fava*

According to Rena Salaman, this dip is probably the same pulse porridge with olive oil called *etnos* that was favoured by Hercules and sold on the streets of ancient Athens. In Greece, it is made with yellow split peas, while in Turkey split dried broad beans are used, making the dip much paler in colour. There is also a Moroccan variation called *beyssara*, which is more like a thick soup and is sold on the streets for breakfast.

**serves 4–6**
250g dried peeled split broad beans, soaked overnight in cold water
2 medium onions, peeled and quartered
5 tbsp extra virgin olive oil
1 tsp caster sugar
2–3 tbsp dill leaves
juice of 1 lemon, or to taste
sea salt

Drain the beans, rinse under cold water and put into a large saucepan. Add the quartered onions, 3 tbsp olive oil and the sugar. Pour on 500ml water and place over a medium heat. Bring to the boil, then lower the heat and simmer for 45 minutes or until the beans are very tender and mushy. Stir every now and then, especially towards the end of cooking to make sure they are not sticking.

Transfer the beans to a food processor and blend until very smooth. The mixture should be thick and creamy, a little like yoghurt. Initially, it may appear too runny, but it will thicken as it stands.

Transfer the puréed beans to a bowl and add half of the dill and most of the lemon juice. Season with salt to taste and mix well. Cover and let cool.

Mix the remaining 2 tbsp olive oil with the rest of the lemon juice and a little salt. Taste the dip and adjust the seasoning if necessary. Spoon into a serving bowl and scatter the remaining dill on top (or stir it in if you prefer). Drizzle with the lemony olive oil and serve immediately.

# taramasalata

*taramosalata* ———

This is very easy to make and homemade taramasalata is far superior to anything you can buy. For a fancy version, use grey mullet roe (bottarga), or for a more familiar and cheaper taramasalata, buy smoked cod's roe. Some Greeks add almonds and, of course, breadcrumbs. I like to make mine with only the roe, olive oil and lemon juice.

**serves 4–6**
350g smoked cod's roe (or
   bottarga)
juice of 1¹/₂–2 lemons
250ml extra virgin olive oil

Put the cod's roe (or bottarga) in a food processor with the lemon juice and process until totally pulverised.

Slowly add the olive oil, as if you were making a mayonnaise. Three-quarters of the way through, taste for tartness and add more lemon juice if the mixture is too bland. Then incorporate the rest of the oil.

The taramasalata should have the consistency of a rather soft potato purée. Serve with very good pita or *marqûq* bread.

# nuts &
# seeds

Nuts and seeds have always been indispensable for mezze, not only to nibble as part of the spread, but also to use in various dishes. The Romans thought almonds kept them sober while drinking! Almonds and pine nuts are the most common varieties in cooking; pistachios and hazelnuts are used to a lesser extent.

For cooking, I prefer to use unpeeled organic almonds, which I soak for half an hour or so in boiling water to make them easier to peel. If I am serving almonds as part of a mezze, I either buy them ready roasted and salted or soak unpeeled almonds in cold water overnight, changing the water from time to time, to rehydrate them and make them taste as if they were fresh. Restaurants in Lebanon prepare them like this, serving the nuts on ice cubes to keep them chilled and moist. And I always serve fresh almonds when they're available in the spring. These are scrumptious dipped in salt and eaten whole – the green skin has a wonderful crunch and a slightly tart flavour, the shell is still soft and the nut inside milky. After a month or so, the green skin and shell harden and become inedible.

As for pine nuts, I use the long Mediterranean type, which are more expensive than the smaller Chinese ones, but far better. I remember how we used to collect pine cones in the Lebanese mountain pine forests and shake them to extract the hard shells containing the nuts. When we had gathered enough shells, we would pick up a stone and crack them open. The trick was to hit the shell hard enough to crack it open without crushing the nut inside.

We also picked green walnuts later in the summer, opening the shells in the same way. It took forever to peel the walnuts and we always ended up with black hands, but it was worth it. Fresh walnuts are delectable. As with almonds, you can soak pine nuts, walnuts and other nuts to rehydrate them and freshen the taste.

Pistachio nuts are the third most expensive variety of nuts in the world, after macadamia and pine nuts. They were introduced to the Levant after Alexander the Great's campaign. Like almonds, pistachios are served fresh when in season, during late summer and early autumn, or eaten roasted and salted, or glazed with lemon juice. Pistachios are the only nut that is green throughout and they make a perfect end to mezze as a meal – soaked and peeled, then mixed with fresh pomegranate seeds.

Peanuts, chickpeas and seeds are typically served roasted and salted as part of a mezze spread.

# pine nut tarator
——— *tarator s'nûbar*

**serves 4**
250g pine nuts
1 garlic clove, peeled
juice of 1½ lemons, or to
  taste
sea salt

Tarator has different meanings in different countries. In Lebanon it describes this dip, or one made with tahini (page 28). In Turkey, it is a walnut or hazelnut dip (like the one below), while in Bulgaria it refers to a yoghurt and cucumber soup, not unlike tzatziki (page 27). This tarator has an intriguing and, in a way, refreshing taste.

Put the pine nuts and garlic in a food processor and process until very fine. With the motor running, slowly and alternately, add the lemon juice and 80–100ml water through the funnel, as if you were making mayonnaise.

The dip should be creamy but not very thick. Transfer to a bowl and add salt to taste. Serve with crudités, or grilled or fried fish.

# walnut tarator
——— *turkish tarator*

**serves 4–6**
100g walnuts
100g soft breadcrumbs
1 garlic clove, peeled
juice of 2 lemons, or to
  taste
2 tbsp extra virgin olive oil
sea salt

This is more substantial than its Lebanese equivalent (above), made a little thicker with breadcrumbs and olive oil. You can vary the flavour by replacing the walnuts with lightly toasted hazelnuts if you like.

Put the walnuts, breadcrumbs and garlic in a food processor and process finely. With the motor still running, slowly add the lemon juice, then 150ml water and finally the olive oil, as if you were making mayonnaise. You should end up with a creamy dip, the consistency of strained yoghurt.

Transfer to a bowl and season with salt to taste. Serve with Turkish mussel brochettes (page 120), crudités or steamed or boiled vegetables, or simply with grilled or poached fish.

# peanut and **chickpea** dry dip

*egyptian doqqah* ————————————

**serves 6–8**

1 tbsp coarse sea salt

40g coriander seeds, toasted

50g peanuts, roasted

50g roasted chickpeas (page 9)

2 tbsp dried mint leaves

4 tbsp sesame seeds, toasted

This is a dry dip. Most people think that you have to dip bread in oil before you dip it in *doqqah* but the Egyptians don't – they scoop up the dry mixture with the bread.

Put the salt, coriander seeds, peanuts and chickpeas in a food processor and grind until medium fine. Transfer to a bowl and stir in the dried mint and sesame seeds. Taste and adjust the salt if necessary. Serve immediately, or store in a sealed jar in a cool, dark cupboard. It will keep for a couple of weeks or so.

# **mackerel** and hazelnut dip

*uskumru taratoru* ————————————

**serves 4–6**

150g hazelnuts (in skins)

3 mackerel fillets (500g)

sea salt

few flat-leaf parsley sprigs

1 small onion, peeled

3 garlic cloves, peeled

45g soft white breadcrumbs

3 tbsp good wine vinegar

*for the garnish*

extra virgin olive oil

sweet paprika

*to serve*

1 lemon, cut into wedges

This is unusual, but delicious – rather more like a spread than a dip. Serve at room temperature or lightly chilled.

Preheat the oven to 180°C/Gas 4. Spread the nuts on a baking tray and roast for 10–15 minutes until lightly toasted. Rub in a clean cloth to remove the skins. Add the mackerel to a shallow pan of barely simmering salted water with the parsley and onion and poach for 4 minutes, or until just done. Remove and flake the fish when cool enough to handle, discarding the skin and any small bones.

Finely grind the nuts and garlic in a food processor, then add the breadcrumbs and 250ml water and whiz until very creamy. Tip into a bowl and stir in the fish, wine vinegar and salt to taste.

Spoon the dip on to a serving plate. Make grooves here and there, drizzle with olive oil and sprinkle with paprika. Serve with lemon wedges.

# harissa

*harissah*

**makes two 500ml jars**
275g dried guajillo peppers
30g dried arbol peppers
50g caraway seeds
20 garlic cloves, peeled
sea salt
extra virgin olive oil, to
    cover

In Tunisia, harissa is eaten as a dip, drizzled with olive oil and sometimes garnished with canned tuna and olives. It is brought to the table before other food, for diners to dip their bread in. I like to use seared fresh tuna as a garnish. Harissa that you buy ready-made, especially in tubes, is quite different, so it is well worth finding good chilli peppers to make your own. I use a mixture of dried Mexican guajillo and arbol peppers to approximate the mild heat of Tunisian peppers.

Pull off the stalks of the dried peppers, shake out and discard the seeds, then rinse under cold water. Now soak the peppers in a bowl of boiling water for about 20 minutes to soften them.

Whiz the caraway seeds in a food processor for a minute or so. Add the garlic and a little salt and process until the garlic is crushed. Drain the peppers and add to the food processor with a little more salt. Process until you have a lightly textured paste – the peppers shouldn't be completely pulverised. Check the seasoning, adding a little more salt if necessary.

Spoon into two 500ml glass jars and cover with a layer of olive oil. Each time you use some of the harissa, you will need to top up the oil. Harissa will keep for a few months in the fridge if it is well covered with oil.

# tabbûlé &
# other salads

# thyme and rocket salad

*————— salatet za'tar wa roqqa*

This is a classic Lebanese late summer mezze. The fresh thyme used here is available from Lebanese shops in the summer and early autumn and is quite different from the familiar herb. If unobtainable, use all wild rocket instead. The secret is to dress the salad at the last minute, so the leaves don't go soggy.

**serves 4–6**
250g fresh thyme on the stalk, leaves only
100g wild rocket
1 small Spanish onion, peeled and very finely chopped
2 tsp sumac, or to taste
3 tbsp extra virgin olive oil
sea salt

Combine the thyme, rocket and onion in a salad bowl. Add the sumac and olive oil and toss well. Taste to see if you need to add any salt – I have a sneaking suspicion that some sumac brands have added salt as saltiness seems to vary. Adjust the seasoning if necessary. Serve immediately.

# rocket with tomatoes

*————— salatet roqqa wa banadûrah*

**serves 4–6**
120g wild rocket
12 cherry tomatoes
juice of 1/2 lemon, or to
 taste
2 tbsp extra virgin olive oil
sea salt

Rocket, also known as *arugula*, *rucola* and *roquette*, has been gathered in the wild in the Mediterranean since Roman times, but has only recently been cultivated on a large scale. Wild rocket is nice served on its own, but it is even better paired with tomato, which is the perfect sweet foil to its sharp taste. Be sure to dress the salad just before serving so that it does not wilt.

Put the rocket leaves in a bowl. Quarter the cherry tomatoes and remove the seeds. Add the tomatoes to the rocket with the lemon juice, olive oil and salt to taste. Toss carefully, then taste and adjust the seasoning if necessary. Serve immediately.

# tabbûlé

*tabbûleh*

**serves 4–6**
30g fine burghul
600g firm ripe tomatoes
50g spring onions, trimmed
400g flat-leaf parsley, most
   of the stalk removed
70g mint sprigs, leaves
   only
1/4 tsp ground cinnamon
1/2 tsp Lebanese 7-spice
   mixture (or ground
   allspice)
1/4 tsp finely ground black
   pepper
sea salt
juice of 1 lemon, or to taste
150ml extra virgin olive oil
4 gem lettuce, washed and
   quartered

Tabbûlé is a global salad now – served everywhere, from corner delis to fancy restaurants. In some places it is made as it would be in Lebanon, where it is one of the few national dishes. In other places, it is so different that you wouldn't know you were eating tabbûlé, except by name. I only wish chefs would give these creations another name. There are authentic variations however, as you will discover overleaf.

Rinse the burghul in several changes of cold water. Drain well and put into a bowl. While you prepare the other ingredients, stir the burghul with a fork every now and then to fluff it up.

Dice the tomatoes into small cubes, tip them into a bowl and set aside. Slice the spring onions into thin rounds. Don't use a mezzaluna to chop the herbs as this will produce a mush. Instead, gather as much as you can handle in a bunch and, with a razor-sharp knife, slice the bunched herbs very thinly, as if you were shaving them, to produce nice, crisp thin strips. Tip the chopped herbs into a large bowl.

Drain the tomatoes of their juice and add them to the herbs. Add the spring onions and burghul. Season with the cinnamon, spice mix or allspice, pepper and salt to taste. Drizzle over the lemon juice and olive oil and toss well. Taste and adjust the seasoning if necessary. Serve with the gem lettuce.

**note** Draining the diced tomatoes of their juice before adding them to the salad will make your tabbûlé quite crisp and keep it fresh for longer.

# white tabbûlé

*——tabbûleh baidah*

**serves 4–6**
100g fine burghul
1 organic pointed white
  cabbage, about 500g
400g firm ripe tomatoes
100g spring onions,
  trimmed and thinly sliced
200g mint, leaves only,
  chopped quite finely
juice of 1 lemon, or to taste
100ml extra virgin olive oil
$\frac{1}{2}$ tsp paprika
sea salt and freshly ground
  black pepper

I am not sure where this version of tabbûlé originates from, but I suspect it may be a regional variation. The white cabbage gives the salad a delicious crunch.

Rinse the burghul in several changes of cold water. Drain and set aside to fluff up, stirring with a fork every now and then to separate the grains.

Discard the outermost leaves from the cabbage, then shred it very finely and place in a large bowl. Halve, deseed and dice the tomatoes and add to the cabbage with the spring onions and chopped mint.

Sprinkle over the burghul and add the lemon juice and olive oil. Season with the paprika and salt and pepper to taste and toss to mix. Taste and adjust the seasoning and lemon juice if necessary. Serve immediately.

# rice tabbûlé

*——tabbûleh rezz*

This tabbûlé is similar to the classic one on the previous page, except that the burghul is replaced with basmati rice.

Soak 200g basmati rice in salted water for 2 hours. Drain the rice, tip into a pan of boiling water and boil for 3 minutes. Drain and spread out on a clean tea towel to dry. Make a classic tabbûlé (page 45), using the rice in place of burghul.

**note** To add a nice crunch to the tabbûlé, you can toss the blanched and dried rice with a little olive oil to coat, then spread out on a baking tray and toast it lightly in a moderate oven at 180°C/Gas 4 for 20–30 minutes until slightly crisp and golden before adding to the salad.

# turkish **burghul** salad

*kissir* ————————————

Kissir is the Turkish version of tabbûlé, with burghul as the main ingredient rather than parsley, and it may well be responsible for the misconception of tabbûlé in the west. Only relatively recently have people in this country begun to realise that tabbûlé is a herb salad, and not a grain salad like this one. Nevertheless, this burghul salad is just as scrumptious and healthy, with an intriguing sweet and sour taste from the dressing.

Put the burghul into a large bowl and gradually stir in 200ml boiling water. Cover the bowl with a tea towel and leave to stand for 15 minutes.

In the meantime, chop the onions very finely. Halve and deseed the tomatoes and cut into 1cm cubes. Trim, deseed and finely dice the green pepper.

When the standing time is up, add the onions to the burghul and mix well. Add the tomatoes, green pepper and parsley, then the olive oil, pomegranate syrup and seasonings. Toss well. Taste and adjust the seasoning if necessary. Serve immediately.

**note** If you do not have any pomegranate syrup, use lemon juice, which will provide a more straightforward, tart flavour.

**serves 4–6**
200g finely ground burghul
2 small Spanish onions, peeled
5 medium firm ripe tomatoes, about 500g
1/2 small green pepper
25g flat-leaf parsley, most of the stalk removed, finely chopped
4 tbsp extra virgin olive oil
1 1/2 tbsp pomegranate syrup (or 3 tbsp lemon juice)
sea salt
1 tsp Aleppo pepper

# olives &
# olive oil

Olives and olive oil are key items in the mezze larder. Olive oil is used in cooking, for dressing salads and for drizzling over dips and other dishes, while olives are an essential part of the mezze table.

I use a fine extra virgin olive oil to dress salads and for drizzling over dishes – ideally a single estate, cold pressed oil. For cooking, I use a mild extra virgin olive oil, which I buy in 5 litre cans to decant into a bottle as and when I need it. Buying oil in cans reminds me of my mother buying olive oil in Lebanon. She never bought commercially produced oil – she didn't trust it to be good enough. Instead, we got our yearly supply from my uncle who owned large olive groves. He brought us the oil in big cans and my mother would then decant it into large straw-covered glass bottles.

In Lebanon, we have three grades of extra virgin olive oil, all of which are pressed from hand picked olives. *Khadir* (green) is pressed from totally unblemished green olives; *bab awwal* (first door) is pressed from slightly blemished olives; *bab thani* (second door) is the oil extracted from the rest of the crop. As for the olives that fall on the ground, they are pressed to use in soap-making. You will probably come across this kind of grading in other olive oil producing countries.

Good storage is key to keeping your olive oil in perfect condition. Keep the oil away from both light and heat. It is no good having wonderful olive oil bottled in a dark glass bottle if you are going to store it in a hot cabinet, or leave it by the cooker.

As for olives, there are plenty to choose from. You have good olives in Lebanon, Greece, Italy, Spain, France, Tunisia and Morocco. In each of these countries, you will find different varieties, but there are only two basic types. Green olives are fully developed but not yet ripe, while black or purple olives are completely ripe. Olives can be cured in salt, brine or olive oil. Whichever variety you choose, don't buy them already pitted – often these are more like rubber than olives. If you like your olives stoned, you can buy any one of several great gadgets that pit olives in no time.

In London, I tend to buy my olives from Middle Eastern shops, but I also like to buy them on my travels: giant green olives with a lovely crunch from Puglia, Sicily or Spain; tiny tasty picholine olives from the south of France; fleshy purple olives from Morocco. Often I enhance the flavour of shop-bought olives by adding dried herbs and citrus peel, or chopped garlic, tiny peeled lemon segments, chilli and good olive oil.

# feta cheese salad

*————— çingene pilavi*

This scrumptious salad is also wonderful served in bread, such as triangles of sesame pita (see right). Or you can wrap it in *marqûq* or pita and cut it into bite-sized pieces to serve as Lebanese 'sushi'. The salad also makes an excellent topping for bruschetta-style mezze (page 69).

**serves 4**
1 Turkish marmara pepper (see note)
1 medium red onion, peeled and finely diced
2 firm, ripe medium tomatoes on the vine
200g feta cheese
1–2 tbsp finely chopped flat-leaf parsley,
  plus extra for garnish
3 tbsp extra virgin olive oil
sea salt (if required)

Halve, core, deseed and thinly slice the pepper. Place in a large bowl with the diced onion. Halve and deseed the tomatoes, then cut into small cubes or thin slices and add to the bowl. Dice the feta and add to the salad with the chopped parsley.

Drizzle over the olive oil and toss the salad carefully. Taste for seasoning – some feta is quite salty and you may not need any salt. Transfer to a serving dish, scatter over some more parsley and serve at room temperature.

**note** If you cannot find the Turkish marmara peppers, use a small bell pepper and dice it quite small.

# grilled aubergine salad

—————— *salatet el-raheb*

**serves 4–6**

4 medium aubergines,
  about 250g each
12 cherry tomatoes
1 small Spanish onion,
  peeled and finely chopped
2–3 mint sprigs, leaves
  only, finely shredded
1 garlic clove, peeled and
  crushed
sea salt
juice of 1½ lemons, or to
  taste
3 tbsp extra virgin olive oil

The key to success here is the quality of the aubergines – they should be very firm, with as few seeds as possible. Large Italian purple aubergines, which are available here in the summer, are ideal. Make sure you grill them as close to the heat source as possible in order to char the skin and get the smoky flavour.

Preheat the grill to high (or prepare the barbecue ready for cooking). Prick the aubergines with the tip of a sharp knife in several places, to stop the skin from bursting during grilling. Grill or barbecue, turning them regularly to expose all sides to the heat, until the aubergines are very soft to the touch and the skin is quite blackened in parts. Depending on the intensity of the heat, this may take 30–50 minutes.

Transfer the aubergines to a board and cut in half lengthways. Scoop out the flesh from the skins and place in a colander. Leave for at least half an hour to drain off the excess liquid.

Cut the aubergine flesh into chunks and place in a salad bowl. Quarter and deseed the cherry tomatoes, then cut each quarter in half. Add to the aubergines with the onion, mint, garlic and salt to taste.

Drizzle over the lemon juice and olive oil and carefully toss, so as to avoid mushing the aubergines. Check the seasoning. Serve warm or at room temperature.

# moroccan
# **aubergine** salad
*za'lûq* —————

**serves 4–6**

2 medium aubergines,
  about 200g each
3 garlic cloves, peeled
5 tbsp extra virgin olive oil
2 x 400g cans cherry
  tomatoes, drained
100g coriander sprigs,
  most of the stalk removed,
  finely chopped
$1/2$ tsp ground cumin
juice of $1/2$ lemon, or to
  taste
$1/8$ tsp dried chilli flakes
$1/8$ tsp finely ground black
  pepper
sea salt
$1/4$ tsp paprika

There is no tradition of mezze as such in Morocco. The nearest to it would be *salades variées*, a variety of salads that are on the table throughout the meal, for diners to nibble on and refresh their palate between bites or courses. These salads are a wonderful, if unorthodox addition to a mezze spread. This one can be made with fried or boiled aubergines, or with steamed aubergines, which is my favourite version.

Peel the aubergines lengthways, removing strips of skin to create a striped effect. Quarter lengthways and slice across into 1cm thick pieces. Put the aubergine pieces and garlic cloves in a steamer and steam for 30 minutes, or until very soft.

Put the olive oil in a sauté pan over a medium-high heat. Add the tomatoes, coriander and cumin and stir well. Cook for about 15 minutes, stirring occasionally, until the excess juices have evaporated and the sauce looks fresh and chunky.

Lightly mash the cooked aubergines and garlic with a fork or a potato masher – don't use a food processor or the aubergines will become too mushy. The salad should have a soft, but chunky texture.

Add the aubergines to the tomato sauce together with the lemon juice, chilli flakes, pepper and salt to taste. Mix well and simmer over a low heat for another 15 minutes, stirring regularly. Add the paprika, then taste and adjust the seasoning if necessary. Serve at room temperature.

# moroccan
# **carrot** salad

*———————— khizû m'rqed*

Many Moroccan salads are ideal to include in a modern mezze spread. This one is healthy, but not in any way dull. Its classic dressing is spiced with $1^1/_2$ tsp each ground paprika and cumin, but I prefer to use chilli and fresh herbs when the salad is part of a mezze spread, as these simpler flavours are easier to marry with other dishes.

**serves 4–6**
750g baby carrots (preferably Chantenay)
3 garlic cloves, peeled
coarse sea salt

*for the seasoning*
2 tbsp finely chopped flat-leaf parsley
2 tbsp finely chopped coriander
$1/_2$ tsp dried chilli flakes
$1^1/_2$ tbsp champagne wine vinegar
4 tbsp extra virgin olive oil

Peel and trim the carrots and place in a saucepan with the garlic cloves. Add water to cover and bring to the boil over a medium heat. Add salt to taste and lower the heat. Boil gently for 7–8 minutes, or until the carrots are just tender. Drain and discard the garlic cloves. Spread the carrots out on a clean tea towel and leave to cool slightly.

Combine the ingredients for the seasoning in a salad bowl and whisk together to combine. Add the carrots and toss gently until they are evenly coated. Taste and add salt if needed. Serve immediately, or at room temperature.

Using tahini as the basis for a salad dressing may be unfamiliar in the west but in Lebanon it is quite common. A diluted tahini dip is often used to dress cooked vegetables, such as beetroot, chard stalks, potatoes or colocassia.

# beetroot salad with tahini

*salatet shmandar bil-tahineh*

**serves 4–6**
800g medium beetroot
2 tbsp finely chopped flat-leaf parsley
tahini dip (page 28), diluted with a little water or
  lemon juice

Preheat the oven to 200°C/Gas 6. Trim the beetroot stalks, but be careful to avoid cutting into the vegetable, otherwise it will bleed during roasting. Wash and drain the beetroot, then wrap each one in foil. Place on a baking sheet and roast in the oven for about 1¹/₂ hours, or until cooked.

Unwrap the beetroot and peel, while still hot. Let cool for a while, then slice across into thin rounds, about 3mm thick. Arrange the slices in overlapping circular rows on a platter.

Stir the chopped parsley into the diluted tahini dip. Drizzle a little over the beetroot. Serve immediately, with the rest of the tahini dressing on the side.

# moroccan **cucumber** salad

—— *khiyar mehqûq*

**serves 4**

3 regular cucumbers (about 1kg)
sea salt
1 1/2 tbsp icing sugar, sifted
1 tbsp thyme leaves
1 1/2 tbsp white wine vinegar
1/2 tsp ground caraway seeds

Here is an unusual way to dress a salad – no oil, just vinegar and sugar for a sweet-sour flavour. The caraway seeds and thyme add a piquant note. A lovely, refreshing summer mezze to serve with arak.

Peel the cucumbers, leaving on very thin strips of skin. Halve lengthways, scoop out the seeds, then grate coarsely. Place the cucumber in a colander, sprinkle with a little salt and mix well. Leave for 30 minutes, then squeeze to get rid of excess liquid.

Place the grated cucumber in a salad bowl. and add the icing sugar, thyme, wine vinegar and caraway. Mix well, then taste and adjust the seasoning if necessary. Serve slightly chilled.

# **cabbage** salad

—— *salatet malfûf*

**serves 4–6**

600g white cabbage
1 garlic clove, peeled and crushed
few leaves fresh mint, very thinly shredded
200g firm ripe tomatoes, deseeded and diced (optional)
sea salt
juice of 1 lemon, or to taste
4 tbsp extra virgin olive oil

This refreshing salad is is one of my favourites. In the summer, I use the imported tender-leaf, flat-topped cabbage sold in Middle Eastern shops, otherwise I buy an organic pointed cabbage.

Discard any damaged outer leaves from the cabbage, then quarter and remove the core. Shred the leaves very finely, using a sharp knife or the fine slicer attachment of a food processor. Place in a salad bowl. Add the garlic, mint, tomatoes if using and salt to taste. Drizzle over the lemon juice and olive oil and toss well. Check the seasoning.

Serve the salad immediately, or let stand for 15–30 minutes and you will find the flavour improves, but not if left for longer.

# grilled pepper salad
## *chakchûka* ————————

**serves 4–6**
4 yellow (or red) peppers
3 tbsp extra virgin olive oil
3 x 400g cans cherry tomatoes, drained
2 garlic cloves, peeled and crushed
scant $1/2$ tsp dried chilli flakes
1 tsp paprika
sea salt
1 preserved lemon, peel only, cut into strips
50g flat-leaf parsley, most of the stalk removed,
   finely chopped

Here is another wonderful Moroccan salad, which is traditionally made using long, thin-fleshed green peppers with a slightly piquant flavour – similar to the Turkish marmara peppers. I prefer to use yellow (or red) bell peppers, which would be frowned upon by most Moroccans, but they're sweeter and make for a prettier presentation.

Preheat the grill to high. Place the peppers on the grill rack and grill for 20–30 minutes, turning occasionally, until the skin is charred and blistered on all sides and the flesh is soft. Let cool a little, then peel the peppers. Cut in half and discard the seeds and core, then slice into medium-thin strips.

Put the olive oil in a large frying pan over a medium-high heat. Add the tomatoes, garlic, chilli flakes, paprika and salt to taste. Cook for 15–20 minutes, stirring occasionally, until all excess liquid has evaporated and the sauce is thick, fresh and chunky.

Add the grilled peppers, preserved lemon and chopped parsley to the tomato sauce. Cook, stirring occasionally, for a further 5–10 minutes until the sauce is very concentrated. Serve at room temperature.

# herb and toasted pita salad

*———————— fattûsh*

*Fattûsh* is becoming increasingly popular here and, as with tabbûlé, the versions you are likely to come across tend to be quite different from those eaten in Lebanon and Syria. An authentic *fattûsh* doesn't necessarily include lettuce, and the bread may be soaked in the dressing, or even fried as it is in Syria before mixing into the salad – keeping it crisp but making the salad rather unhealthy. I achieve crispness by tossing the bread with the sumac and olive oil before mixing it into the salad – the oil coats the bread and protects it from the juices for longer.

Open up the pita bread at the seam, so you have two discs. Toast until golden brown on both sides, then break into bite-sized pieces and place in a bowl. Sprinkle the sumac all over the toasted pita pieces, then add the olive oil and toss well.

Remove any damaged outer leaves from the lettuce, then cut across into 1cm strips. If using a regular cucumber, peel, quarter lengthways and deseed; if using small cucumbers, simply halve lengthways. Cut the cucumber(s) across into slices. Thinly slice the spring onions. Chop the tomatoes into bite-sized pieces. Put these ingredients into a large salad bowl.

Add the herbs to the salad and season with salt to taste. Add the seasoned bread and toss well. Taste and adjust the seasoning if necessary. Serve immediately.

**serves 6**
1 medium pita bread
3 tbsp sumac
6 tbsp extra virgin olive oil
400g gem lettuce
300g cucumbers
  (preferably small Middle
  Eastern cucumbers)
100g spring onions,
  trimmed
300g firm red tomatoes
200g flat-leaf parsley, most
  of the stalk removed,
  coarsely chopped
100g mint, leaves only,
  coarsely chopped
100g purslane, leaves only
sea salt

Unusual ingredients are increasingly finding a place on supermarket shelves, though you are still more likely to find purslane (a fragile herb) and *meqteh* (small cucumbers) in Middle Eastern shops. They are in season during late summer and early autumn. *Meqteh* is better known in the US where it goes by the name of Armenian cucumber, despite the fact that it isn't Armenian. *Meqteh* is quite different from normal cucumber. The skin is ridged, slightly furry and much paler in colour. Also the shape is different: longer, thinner and often curved. As for the texture, it is crunchier and less watery.

# purslane, tomato and cucumber salad

*salatet baqleh, banadûrah wa meqteh*

**serves 4**
200g *meqteh* (Armenian cucumbers), thinly sliced
100g spring onions, trimmed and thinly sliced
200g tomatoes, quartered and deseeded
500g purslane, leaves only
juice of ¹/₂ lemon
sea salt
3 tbsp extra virgin olive oil

Put the sliced cucumbers, spring onions and tomatoes in a salad bowl. Toss to mix, then add the purslane. Add the lemon juice, salt to taste and the olive oil. Toss lightly together. Taste and adjust the seasoning if necessary. Serve immediately.

**note** You can vary the dressing for this salad if you like, by using 1 tbsp sumac instead of the lemon juice.

savoury pastries
& mini wraps

# za'tar bites

*———— manaqish loqmeh*

**makes about 42–48**
600g block ready-made
  puff pastry
flour, for dusting

*for the topping*
5$\frac{1}{2}$ tbsp za'tar (page 107)
5$\frac{1}{2}$ tbsp extra virgin
  olive oil

Preheat the oven to 220°C/Gas 7. For the topping, mix the za'tar with the olive oil in a small bowl and set aside.

Roll out the pastry on a lightly floured surface to a 45 x 35cm rectangle. Using a 5cm pastry cutter, cut out as many discs as you can (at least 42). Work quickly to keep the pastry cool. Transfer to a non-stick baking sheet.

Spread just under $\frac{1}{2}$ tsp za'tar mixture on each pastry disc, leaving a clear margin around the edge – the topping should spread to cover the top during baking, without dribbling over the sides. Bake for 20–25 minutes, or until well puffed and golden brown. Transfer to a wire rack to cool. Serve warm or at room temperature.

## variations

**spicy lamb bites** For the topping, put 1 very finely chopped onion in a bowl, add salt and rub with your fingers to soften. Add 150g lean minced lamb, 1 deseeded and diced tomato, 1 tsp lemon juice, $\frac{1}{4}$ tsp each ground cinnamon and cayenne, $\frac{1}{2}$ tsp ground allspice, a pinch of pepper and more salt if needed. Mix well. Make the bites as above, using about $\frac{1}{2}$ tsp meat mixture to top each pastry disc (in place of the za'tar). Scatter over a few pine nuts before baking.

**aubergines bites** Put 3 tbsp olive oil, $\frac{1}{2}$ diced red pepper and 1 diced medium aubergine in a pan, season and cook gently, covered, for 15 minutes. Add 1 crushed garlic clove, 400g can cherry tomatoes, drained, and a pinch of dried chilli flakes. Cook, covered, for a further 15 minutes until well reduced. Add some finely chopped parsley and coriander and cook, uncovered, for 5 minutes or so, until no excess liquid remains. Let cool. Make and bake the bites as above, using $\frac{1}{2}$–$\frac{3}{4}$ tsp topping for each (in place of the za'tar).

In Lebanon, *manaqish* are eaten as breakfast pizzas, but here I have reduced them to bite-size to serve as mezze. I've also used puff pastry in place of the usual bread base. Topped with za'tar speckled with sesame seeds, they not only look gorgeous, they taste scrumptious.

# lebanese bruschetta

*toast labneh* —————

**serves 4–6**

3 thin slices poîlane bread, or other good sourdough

250g labné (see note)

15 green olives, pitted and coarsely chopped, plus extra for garnish

few mint sprigs, leaves only, finely chopped, plus extra for garnish

sea salt

2–3 tbsp extra virgin olive oil

toasted sesame seeds, for garnish

I love bruschetta and thought it would be fun to adapt the concept to mezze. Instead of topping the bread the Italian way, I use typical Lebanese or Turkish sandwich fillings. This recipe calls for a labné topping, but you can vary it by using za'tar (page 14), feta cheese salad (page 50) or aubergine salad (pages 52–3). If you use za'tar, grill the bruschettas for a minute or so until the topping is bubbling. I make my own labné, usually with goat's milk yoghurt – it's very easy to do (see note).

Toast the bread until golden on both sides and cut each slice into 3 or 4 pieces. Let cool on a wire rack. Meanwhile, put the labné into a bowl, add the olives and chopped mint and mix well. Season with salt to taste, then add the olive oil and mix lightly – you should still see trails of oil.

Spoon the labné mixture on to the toast slices. Garnish some of the bruschettas with toasted sesame seeds, some with mint and the rest with chopped olives. Serve immediately.

**note** To make your own labné, you will need twice the quantity of goat's milk or sheep's milk yoghurt to the amount of labné specified. Pour the yoghurt into a muslin-lined colander, bring up the corners of the muslin and tie to form a sack, then slip the handles over the tap of your kitchen sink. Leave overnight to allow the excess liquid to drain off. The next morning, you'll have a better, thicker labné than any you will find in the shops.

# filo & other pastries

Filo is the name that Greeks use to describe dough – any kind – not just the very thin sheets of dough that we refer to as filo (or phyllo). Despite the familiarity of the Greek name, the filo we know originated in Turkey. As long ago as the 11th century its Turkish equivalent – *yurgha* (now *yufka*) – was described as 'pleated/folded bread' in a dictionary of local dialect.

Before the 1st World War, elegant households in Istanbul kept two filo-makers, one to make thin sheets for baklava and the other to make the thicker sheets used in böreks. This is not so common nowadays, but many traditional households in Turkey still make filo at home. It is fascinating to watch, but very time-consuming, so I always buy it ready-made.

You can find excellent filo in Middle Eastern shops and very good *yufka* in Turkish shops. Filo sheets tear easily and dry very quickly if they are not kept covered, whereas *yufka* is easier to work with because it is slightly thicker and pre-cooked. I usually keep my filo sheets covered with cling film and then a tea towel.

*Warqa* is the Moroccan equivalent of these pastries and like *yufka*, it is pre-cooked. It is prepared by slightly overlapping circles of very wet dough on a lightly oiled hot plate to produce a large, round, fine sheet of pliable pastry. Because *warqa* is slightly oiled and partly cooked, it is more pliable and dries less quickly. Good filo, *yufka* and *warqa* should all be very thin and are interchangeable in my *fatayer* and börek recipes (pages 72–7).

As for puff pastry, it is made by a complex process of folding dough to encase butter, then rolling out the dough, folding it again, turning it and rolling out again. The folding, turning and rolling process is done six times, and the dough is allowed to rest in between each time. As it bakes, the pastry puffs up and separates in hundreds of ultra thin layers, hence its French name: *pâte feuilletée*.

The best puff is made with butter, but unfortunately margarine is used in most ready-prepared brands. I tend to buy my puff pastry from a good baker. (You can buy excellent puff pastry in blocks from Sally Clarke's in London.) Ready-made puff pastry is easy to use. The key to success is to flour the pastry liberally when you are rolling it out so that it doesn't stick and to work quickly so it stays cold.

I suggest using these ready-made doughs in my recipes rather than the more traditional doughs because it makes the preparation of the various pastries easier and quicker. The texture may be different, but the taste remains authentic.

# spinach filo parcels
—— *fatayer bil-sabanegh*

*Fatayer* are typical Syrian/ Lebanese mezze, made here with filo rather than the traditional dough. They can be filled with greens (spinach, purslane or Swiss chard), labné, cheese, eggs or courgette, to name but a few options. And you can make larger or smaller triangles, or shape rolls if you prefer.

**serves 6–8**
1 x 400g packet filo pastry (about 14 sheets)
125g unsalted butter, melted

*for the filling*
1 medium onion, peeled and very finely chopped
sea salt
1/2 tsp finely ground black pepper
2 tbsp sumac
400g spinach, well washed
2 tbsp pine nuts
juice of 1 lemon, or to taste
2 tbsp extra virgin olive oil

To make the filling, put the onion in a small bowl. Add a little salt, the pepper and sumac and, with your fingers, rub the seasonings into the onion to soften it.

Shred the spinach and place in a large bowl. Sprinkle with a little salt and rub in with your hands until the spinach is wilted. Squeeze the spinach very dry. Transfer to a clean bowl and separate the leaves. Add the onion with the pine nuts, lemon juice and olive oil. Mix well, then taste and adjust the seasoning – the filling should be strongly flavoured to offset the bland pastry. Tip into a sieve and leave to drain off the excess juices.

Preheat the oven to 200°C/Gas 6. Lay one filo sheet on a work surface and cut across in half; keep the others covered so that they don't dry out. Brush each filo length with butter and fold in half lengthways. Now fill and shape according to the instructions overleaf. Trim any loose ends. Brush both sides with butter, then place on a non-stick baking sheet, loose side down. Cover with cling film and make the rest of the triangles in the same way. You should end up with 28.

Bake the triangles for 15–25 minutes, or until crisp and golden brown all over. Transfer to a wire rack to cool a little before serving. They are best eaten warm or at room temperature.

## variations
**spicy cheese filo parcels**  For the filling, use 500g feta cheese seasoned with 2 tsp Aleppo pepper. Shape and bake as above. Serve hot from the oven.

**labné filo parcels**  For the filling, put 1 very finely chopped large onion in a bowl, add salt and rub with your fingers to soften. Add 3/4 tsp each ground cinnamon and allspice, 1/3 tsp pepper, 3 diced small tomatoes, 450g labné (page 69) and 1 tbsp softened butter. Mix well and season with more salt if needed. Shape and bake as above. Serve hot from the oven.

### shaping a filo triangle

Brush the filo strip with butter, then place 1½ tbsp of filling across the corner nearest to you and fold the other corner over the filling to make a triangle.

Carefully pick up the triangle and fold it over, again and again, keeping the shape, until you reach the end, brushing with butter every two or three folds.

# turkish meat böreks

*kol böregi* ——————

**makes 18–20**

1 x 400g packet filo pastry
  (about 14 sheets)
125g unsalted butter,
  melted

*for the filling*

1½ tbsp extra virgin olive
  oil
½ tsp cumin seeds
1 large onion, peeled and
  finely chopped
2 tbsp pine nuts
1 garlic clove, peeled and
  finely chopped
225g lean minced lamb
½ red romano pepper,
  trimmed and finely diced
½ red chilli, trimmed and
  finely diced (scant 1 tbsp)
200g can peeled tomatoes,
  drained and finely
  chopped
1½ tbsp sultanas
4 tbsp finely chopped flat-
  leaf parsley
2 tbsp finely chopped dill
½ tsp ground allspice
sea salt and freshly ground
  black pepper

Use a Greek or Turkish brand of filo to make these. Both have bigger sheets than the filo you commonly find in supermarkets and they are rolled out noticeably thinner, with less cornflour in between the sheets.

To make the filling, heat the olive oil in a large frying pan over a medium-high heat. Add the cumin seeds and stir until they release their aroma. Add the onion and pine nuts and cook, stirring regularly, until lightly golden. Stir in the garlic. Add the lamb, red pepper and chilli and stir until the meat is no longer pink, pressing it with the back of the spoon to break up any lumps. Add the tomatoes, sultanas, herbs and allspice, and season with salt and pepper. Cook for a few minutes, stirring occasionally, until all of the liquid has evaporated. Let cool.

Preheat the oven to 200°C/Gas 6. Lay one filo sheet on your work surface. Keep the others covered with cling film, then a tea towel so that they don't dry out. Brush the filo sheet with melted butter, then cut it across in half. Turn both halves around, so you have the cut side nearest to you.

Place 2 tsp filling in a thin line across the end nearest to you, leaving 1.5cm free at the edges and from the top. Carefully fold the filo over the filling and roll, brushing with melted butter every two or three folds, to make a thin cylinder. Flatten one end, fold it over and roll the cylinder to make a coil. Brush with butter on both sides. Tuck the loose plain end under the coil and place on a non-stick baking sheet. Make the other coils in the same way and transfer to the baking sheet.

Bake in the oven for 15–20 minutes, or until the böreks are golden brown all over. Serve hot or warm.

# lebanese potato and basil wrap

— *arûss batata ma' habaq*

**serves 4–6**

500g potatoes, scrubbed
  and rinsed
sea salt
6 tbsp extra virgin olive oil,
  plus extra for brushing
30g basil sprigs, leaves
  only, finely chopped
1 medium Spanish onion,
  peeled and very finely
  chopped
freshly ground black
  pepper
2 *marqûq* breads

A Lebanese sandwich is basically a wrap made with one layer of thin pita or two layers of *marqûq* bread and a tasty filling, such as the basil-flavoured mash below, or *qashqawan* (a hard ewe's milk cheese), or labné mixed with olive oil and spring onions. This wrap was one of my favourite snacks as a child.

Halve or quarter the potatoes, put into a pan and cover with water. Bring to the boil, add salt and boil gently for 20 minutes, or until the potatoes are done. Drain and place in a large bowl. Mash the potatoes with a fork or a potato masher. Add the olive oil, basil and onion and mix well. Season with pepper to taste and more salt if necessary.

Trim the breads to make squares, the sides measuring about 35cm. Fold one bread in half and brush with olive oil. Spread half the potato mash across the bread leaving about 1cm free around the edges. Then fold the long edge nearest to you over the potatoes and gently roll to make a cylinder. Cut the cylinder, on the slant, into 4 wraps. Place on a baking sheet, loose side down. Make and divide the other wrap in the same way. Transfer to the baking sheet, loose side down.

At this stage, you can loosely cover the wraps with cling film and set them aside for a couple of hours or a little longer. Just before you are ready to eat, slip them into a very hot oven at 230°C/Gas 8 for 2–3 minutes to crisp the bread up a little. Serve immediately.

# cheese and cucumber wrap

*arûss jibneh ma' khiyar* ——

Here, I suggest you use thin pita rather than *marqûq*, especially if you decide to toast the wraps lightly before serving. You can also cut the roll into smaller pieces, to make a Lebanese version of sushi.

**serves 4–6**
2 medium pita breads
2 organic cucumbers
300g feta cheese
60g mint sprigs, leaves only, finely chopped
4 tbsp extra virgin olive oil, plus extra for brushing

Open the pita bread at the seams to make 4 thin discs. Peel the cucumbers, quarter lengthways and scoop out the seeds, then cut across into thin slices and place in a bowl. Crumble in the feta, add the chopped mint and olive oil and mix well.

Lay one disc of pita bread, textured side up, on your work surface and brush with olive oil. Spread with a quarter of the feta mixture. Roll into a tight cylinder and cut in two on the slant. Transfer to a baking sheet, loose side down. Make the other wraps the same way and transfer to the baking sheet. Cover loosely with cling film.

When you are ready to serve the wraps, slip them into a very hot oven for 2–3 minutes at 230°C/Gas 8 to crisp up the bread. Serve immediately.

# pulses & grains

To me, carrots, lentils and yoghurt are not a natural combination, but they come together to great effect in this Turkish mezze. The recipe belongs to the family of dishes that are cooked in oil, known as *zeytinyaglu* in Turkey and *bil-zeyt* in Arabic.

# carrots and lentils

*zeytinyagli havuç* ———————

Heat the olive oil in a saucepan over a medium-high heat. Add the onions and fry, stirring occasionally, until golden. Stir in the tomato purée, then add the carrots and stir for a minute or so. Take off the heat and set aside.

Drain and rinse the lentils. Put them in a saucepan, add 500ml water and bring to the boil. Lower the heat, cover the pan and simmer for 15 minutes.

Add the lentils and their liquid to the carrots and season with salt and pepper to taste. Cover and simmer for 15 minutes, stirring occasionally. Uncover the pan, raise the heat slightly and boil gently for 2–3 minutes to drive off excess liquid. Check the seasoning. Cover with a tea towel and let cool.

In the meantime, mix the yoghurt with the crushed garlic and salt to taste. Transfer the carrots and lentils to a shallow serving bowl. Spoon the yoghurt on top and garnish with dill to serve.

**serves 4**
3 tbsp extra virgin olive oil
2 medium onions, peeled and finely chopped
1 tbsp tomato purée (paste)
500g carrots, peeled and sliced
100g green lentils, soaked in cold water for 30 minutes
sea salt and freshly ground black pepper
250g Greek style yoghurt
1 garlic clove, peeled and crushed
dill sprigs, for garnish

# broad bean 'risotto'

—— *rezz bil-fûl*

**serves 4–6**
3 tbsp extra virgin olive oil
1 medium onion, peeled
 and very finely chopped
300g white short-grain rice,
 preferably Bomba or
 Calasparra
1/2 tsp ground cinnamon
1/2 tsp Lebanese 7-spice
 mixture (or ground
 allspice)
1/4 tsp finely ground black
 pepper
sea salt
200g frozen peeled broad
 beans, defrosted

The best rice to use here is Bomba or Calasparra, both types of paella rice. Bomba is superior, but it is not so easy to find. As for the broad beans, you can save a lot of time by buying them already peeled in frozen (200g) packs from Persian food shops. Otherwise you will find standard frozen broad beans easier to peel than fresh ones. If you use fresh broad beans, avoid overgrown pods; shell and blanch the beans before peeling.

Heat the olive oil in a saucepan, add the onion and fry over a medium heat, stirring occasionally, until soft and transparent.

Rinse the rice in a sieve under cold running water, then add to the pan and sauté with the onion for a minute or so. Pour in 600ml water and add the spices, pepper and salt to taste. Bring to the boil, lower the heat, cover the pan and simmer for 10 minutes.

Add the broad beans, mix with the rice and simmer for a further 5 minutes. Check the seasoning. Take the pan off the heat, wrap the lid with a tea towel and put it back on the pan. Let stand for 5 minutes.

Stir with a fork to fluff up the rice, then transfer to a serving dish. Serve hot, warm or at room temperature.

# lentils in olive oil

———— *'adass bil-zeyt*

**serves 4–6**

300g brown lentils,
  soaked in water for
  30 minutes
2 medium Spanish onions,
  peeled and finely chopped
few flat-leaf parsley sprigs,
  most of the stalk
  removed, finely chopped
juice of 1 lemon, or to taste
6 tbsp extra virgin olive oil
1/4 tsp sweet paprika
sea salt and freshly ground
  black pepper

For a long time I thought that lentils didn't need soaking, until I read that Nevin Halici, my guru for all things Turkish, recommends soaking them for 30 minutes before cooking. This hydrates and softens them, and as a result the lentils cook quicker, without going mushy – a definite advantage here.

Drain the lentils and put them into a saucepan. Add water to cover by about 3cm and place over a medium heat. Bring to the boil, then lower the heat and let bubble gently for 20–25 minutes, or until the lentils are just done but not mushy. Drain in a colander and transfer to a bowl.

Add the onions and parsley and toss to mix with the lentils. Then add the lemon juice, olive oil and paprika. Season with salt and pepper to taste and mix well. Taste and adjust the seasoning if necessary. Transfer to a serving dish and serve warm or at room temperature.

# smoked
# **wheat** 'risotto'

*frikeh bil-banadûrah* ——

**serves 4**
2 tbsp extra virgin olive oil
1 medium onion, very finely chopped
2 x 400g cans cherry tomatoes, drained
$1/2$ tsp finely ground black pepper
sea salt
200g frikeh
basil leaves, for garnish

Heat the olive oil in a saucepan over a medium heat. Add the onion and fry, stirring occasionally, until golden. Add the tomatoes and bring to the boil, then cover the pan and let bubble gently for 5 minutes. Season with the pepper and some salt, then add the frikeh and 250ml water. Bring to the boil and let bubble for a couple of minutes.

Lower the heat and simmer, covered, for 25 minutes, stirring occasionally, or until the frikeh is done but not completely dry. The consistency should be quite moist, a little like that of an Italian risotto but not as wet. Wrap the lid with a tea towel and replace over the pan. Let stand for 5 minutes.

Serve the 'risotto' hot, warm or at room temperature, garnished with a few basil leaves.

This dish is traditionally made with coarse burghul but I like to make it with frikeh, which is green smoked wheat. Harvested while still green, the wheat is bunched up and passed over an open fire to char it a little and give it a smoky flavour. Then it is hulled and either kept whole or cracked. You can buy frikeh from Lebanese and other Middle Eastern food shops.

# falafel

*ta'miyah*

Falafel originated in Egypt and are now universally popular, although as with tabbûlé, they are much misinterpreted. The Egyptian version is softer than the Lebanese/Syrian version, perhaps because it is made with only fava beans. I prefer Lebanese falafel, which include chickpeas, though I use rather less of these than most people do.

Drain the chickpeas and broad beans, rinse well and drain them thoroughly. Put into a food processor, add all the rest of the ingredients and process until you have a fine paste. Transfer the mixture to a bowl. Taste and adjust the seasoning if necessary. Cover and let rest in the fridge for 30 minutes.

Pinch off a little falafel mixture and shape between the palms of your hands into a small ball, just smaller than a golf ball. Place on a plate and continue making the falafel until you have used up all the mixture. You should end up with about 20–25 balls.

Heat a 5cm depth of vegetable oil in a large frying pan over a medium heat. To check that the oil is hot enough to deep-fry the falafels, dip in a piece of bread; if the oil bubbles around it, it is ready. Drop in as many balls as will fit comfortably in the pan and deep-fry for 3–4 minutes, turning them every now and then, until golden brown all over.

Using a slotted spoon, remove the falafel and place on several layers of kitchen paper to drain off the excess oil while you cook the rest. Serve them hot or warm, with the tahini dip.

serves 4–6
100g dried chickpeas, soaked in cold water overnight with 1 tsp bicarbonate of soda
200g peeled split dried broad beans, soaked in cold water overnight with 1 tsp bicarbonate of soda
5 large garlic cloves, peeled
1 small onion, peeled and quartered
50g coriander sprigs, most of the stalk discarded
1 tsp ground cumin
1 tsp Lebanese 7-spice mixture (or ground allspice)
1/4 tsp finely ground black pepper
1/8 tsp cayenne pepper
1/2 tsp bicarbonate of soda
sea salt

*to cook and serve*
vegetable oil, for deep-frying
tahini dip (page 28)

# burghul and nut 'burgers'

—————— *batirik*

Most Lebanese dishes have a Turkish equivalent, which is often plainer. These 'burgers' – the Turkish version of southern Lebanese tomato kibbé – are the exception to the rule. They are prettier and rather more elaborate than their Lebanese counterpart, but just as healthy. They can also be made with tahini instead of pistachios, by replacing the nuts with 100ml tahini.

Put the burghul into a bowl. Peel, halve and deseed the tomatoes, then finely chop the flesh. Add to the burghul with the tomato purée and mix well with your hands.

Add the onion and green pepper and mix well, again using your hands. Then mix in the nuts, and finally the chilli pepper, herbs and salt to taste. The mixture should be evenly combined.

Pinch off a handful of the mixture and shape into a round, flat cake about 6cm in diameter. Place on a serving platter. Shape the remaining cakes and arrange on the platter. Sprinkle with a little chopped parsley to garnish and serve immediately.

**serves 4–6**

135g fine burghul
300g firm, ripe tomatoes
1 tsp tomato purée (paste)
1 medium onion, peeled and coarsely grated
1/4 green pepper (about 25g), coarsely grated
100g pistachio nuts, finely ground
1 tsp Aleppo pepper
1 tbsp finely chopped flat-leaf parsley, plus extra for garnish
1 tbsp finely chopped fresh marjoram or oregano
sea salt

# greek giant baked beans

*fasolia gigantes plaki—*

## serves 4

250g *fasolia gigantes* (or butter beans), soaked in cold water for 12 hours with 1 tsp bicarbonate of soda

100ml extra virgin olive oil

2 medium onions, peeled and thinly sliced

2 garlic cloves, peeled and thinly sliced

2 tsp dried oregano

2 tsp fresh thyme leaves

2 x 400g cans cherry tomatoes, drained

2 tsp tomato purée (paste)

sea salt and freshly ground black pepper

2 tbsp finely chopped flat-leaf parsley

This is a healthy, delicious Greek version of baked beans. If you can't find the Greek giant beans, you can use butter beans instead. Indeed, there is a short time in the summer when you can buy fresh butter beans, which are ideal for this dish. If using fresh beans, you will need to use double the quantity.

Drain and rinse the beans. Put them in a saucepan and cover generously with water. Bring to the boil, then lower the heat and simmer for 1 hour, or until the beans are just tender. Drain well and set aside.

Heat the olive oil in a saucepan over a medium-high heat and add the onions and garlic. Fry, stirring occasionally, until golden. Stir in the oregano and thyme, then add the canned tomatoes, tomato purée and seasoning. Let the sauce bubble gently for about 15 minutes, or until thickened.

Meanwhile, preheat the oven to 180°C/Gas 4. Add the parsley and beans to the tomato sauce, mix well, then taste and adjust the seasoning.

Tip the beans and sauce into an ovenproof dish, approximately 24cm in diameter. Bake in the oven for about 30 minutes until the sauce is thickened a little more and the top is crisp and golden – don't stir the beans during baking. Serve hot, warm or at room temperature.

# giant bean salad

*———— salatet fasûliyah 'aridah*

*Alubia judion* are huge Spanish beans. There are different types and all are quite expensive, but you can use butter beans instead here. This salad is even more scrumptious made with fresh butter beans when in season. These are available in Lebanese shops during summer. You can also replace the beans with chickpeas or with small dried broad beans.

**serves 4–6**

250g *alubia judion* (or butter beans), soaked in cold water
  for 12 hours with 1 tsp bicarbonate of soda
1 small garlic clove, peeled and crushed
juice of 1 lemon, or to taste
3 tbsp extra virgin olive oil
2–3 flat-leaf parsley sprigs, most of the stalk discarded,
  finely chopped
sea salt

Drain the beans and rinse well, then put into a large pan and cover well with cold water. Bring to the boil, then lower the heat and simmer for 1 1/2–2 hours, or until the beans are tender but not falling apart. Check every now and then during cooking that the water is still covering them completely.

Drain the beans well and transfer to a salad bowl. Add the garlic, lemon juice, olive oil, chopped parsley and salt to taste. Toss well and serve warm, or at room temperature.

# stuffed, fried &
# other vegetables

# fried okra

—— *bamyeh meqliyeh*

As a child, I always pestered my mother in the kitchen, wanting to see everything that she prepared, but more importantly, wanting to taste it all. I recall how she used to fry okra before cooking it in tomato sauce to stop it releasing its glutinous juices. I loved the delicious crunch of fried okra, so I always pinched a few to eat sprinkled with a little salt. Here I am suggesting you serve fried okra as a mezze, sprinkled with good salt and Aleppo pepper flakes to give them a little kick.

**serves 4–6**
250g okra
4 tbsp extra virgin olive oil
sea salt
Aleppo pepper flakes (or Turkish pepper flakes)

Peel the stem end of the okra, following the slant and making sure you don't cut into the vegetable, otherwise the glutinous juices will seep out during frying. Rinse the okra under cold running water, drain and spread out on a tea towel. Cover with another tea towel and pat dry.

Heat the olive oil in a sauté pan over a medium heat. To test whether the oil is hot enough, dip the tip of an okra pod into the oil; if the oil bubbles around it, then it's ready. Add the okra and sauté for 3–4 minutes until it is bright green, slightly crisp and just done. Transfer to a serving platter.

Sprinkle the fried okra with salt and chilli pepper flakes to taste. Serve immediately.

# moroccan stuffed tomatoes

*———— hadda*

**serves 4–6**
8 medium ripe vine
  tomatoes
5 tbsp extra virgin olive oil,
  plus extra to serve
sea salt
450g firm, medium
  courgettes
1 medium onion, peeled
  and thinly sliced
1 garlic clove, peeled and
  crushed
50g coriander sprigs, most
  of the stalk removed,
  finely chopped
50g flat-leaf parsley, most
  of the stalk removed,
  finely chopped
$1/2$ tsp dried chilli flakes

Preheat the oven to 150°C/Gas 2. Slice the tops off the tomatoes, then scoop out the seeds with a teaspoon and discard. Place the tomatoes upside down on a board to drain. Brush a baking dish large enough to hold them with 1 tbsp olive oil. Stand the tomatoes in the dish, cut side up, and sprinkle with a little salt.

Grate the courgettes and place in a bowl with the onion and garlic. Add the herbs, chilli flakes, 3 tbsp olive oil and salt to taste and mix well. Taste and adjust the seasoning if necessary.

Fill the tomatoes with the courgette mixture, piling it up high in a mound (as illustrated overleaf). Drizzle the remaining olive oil over each tomato. Bake in the oven for $1^{1}/2$–2 hours, or until cooked to your liking – after $1^{1}/2$ hours they will still have a slight crunch.

Spoon the cooking juices over the filling and let cool before transferring to a serving platter. Serve warm or at room temperature, drizzled with a little more olive oil.

**note** For an extra kick, sprinkle the stuffed tomatoes with a little coarsely ground dried chilli just before serving.

The filling for these Moroccan tomatoes is rather unusual in that it is spiced only with chilli, instead of the more usual mix of cumin, paprika, ginger, saffron and other headier spices. The tomatoes make a wonderful, if rather unorthodox mezze, and they taste as good as they look.

# green beans in tomato sauce

———— *lûbyeh bil-zeyt*

This was my favourite dish as a child and the first recipe I ever cooked by myself. When I lived in Beirut, my two sisters and I decided to cook late one night. They chose to make a chocolate cake, while I cooked these beans. Most of the cake ended up in a fight but we ate the beans. I guess that must have been the very start of my cooking career!

**serves 4–6**
400g flat Helda beans, or fine green beans
3 tbsp extra virgin olive oil
1 medium onion, peeled and finely chopped
6 garlic cloves (unpeeled)
sea salt
1 x 400g can cherry tomatoes, drained

Top, tail and, if necessary, string the beans, then cut them on the slant into 5cm pieces; if you are using the fine beans, simply top and tail them. Rinse under cold running water and set aside.

Heat the olive oil in a saucepan over a medium heat. Add the onion and garlic and fry until the onion turns golden. Add the beans and sprinkle with a generous pinch of salt. Cover and cook for a few minutes, stirring regularly, until they turn bright green and become glossy.

Add the tomatoes, season with salt to taste and mix well. Cover the pan and let bubble gently for about 20 minutes until the beans are done to your liking and the sauce is thickened. Serve hot, warm or at room temperature, with pita bread.

# wild chicory in olive oil

*hindbeh bil-zeyt* ——————

For this recipe, you can use frisée if you can't find wild chicory, which is in fact no longer wild but farmed in the Middle East. Frisée is a good substitute, though it is paler and more tender. Even better, when in season, is dandelion (sold in farmers' markets), or cavolo nero. If the dandelion is fully grown, you'll need to allow 10–15 minutes cooking; the same with cavolo nero. An interesting variation here is to add fresh haricot beans.

Bring a pot full of water to the boil, then drop in the chicory or other leaves. Add salt to taste and cook until tender: allow 6 minutes for wild chicory; 3 minutes for frisée; 10–15 minutes for mature dandelion and cavolo nero. Drain the cooked greens and let cool, then squeeze out as much excess liquid as you can, using your hands. Separate the leaves and set aside.

Heat the olive oil in a large frying pan over a medium heat. Add the onions and fry, stirring occasionally, for 15–20 minutes, or until they soften, caramelise and become golden brown.

Add the cooked greens to the pan. Sauté for a few minutes, stirring regularly, until they are well blended with the oil and onions. Add the lemon juice and stir for a minute or so. Taste and adjust the seasoning if necessary. Serve at room temperature, with lemon wedges.

**serves 4**
800g wild chicory, or
  frisée, roughly torn, or
  cavolo nero or dandelion
sea salt
100ml extra virgin olive oil
4 medium onions, peeled
  and thinly sliced
juice of 1 lemon
lemon wedges, to serve

# turkish grilled peppers

*sirkeli sarmisakli biber izgara*

Grilled sweet peppers are a typical Turkish mezze. What makes this version interesting is the simple dressing of vinegar and garlic (but no oil). As it is the dominant flavouring, the choice of vinegar here is important. I often use an aged Greek vinegar made from Corinthian grapes. It has an intense dark colour and a delicate fruity flavour. Otherwise I use champagne vinegar, which has a light colour and an even lighter taste.

**serves 4–6**
8 red peppers
2 garlic cloves, peeled and crushed
6 tbsp good vinegar (see left)
1 tbsp thyme leaves
sea salt

Preheat the grill (or a barbecue). Grill or barbecue the peppers, turning them to expose all sides, for about 25–30 minutes until the skin is charred and the peppers are soft. Lift on to a board and peel off the skin. Cut the peppers open, discard the stem and seeds and slice the flesh into wide pieces. Transfer to a serving platter.

Mix the garlic with the vinegar and most of the thyme leaves, saving some for garnish. Add salt to taste and pour the dressing over the peppers. Leave to stand for about half an hour. Serve at room temperature or slightly chilled, garnished with the reserved thyme leaves.

# fresh &
dried herbs

One of the main attractions of a mezze spread is its freshness. This is partly due to the prolific use of herbs. In the Levant and North Africa herbs often feature as a main ingredient, whereas in the west they are mostly used as a garnish or flavouring.

The predominant herbs in Lebanon and Syria are parsley, mint, coriander, purslane, thyme and basil. In Turkey and Greece, dill is ubiquitous, while in Morocco, coriander and parsley are ever-present, as well as mint of course.

Parsley is native to the eastern Mediterranean and is pre-eminent in the cooking of this part of the world. Indeed, in some dishes, it is used like a vegetable. Flat-leaf parsley is the only variety grown and used, and is at its best when the leaves are still small and tender on thin stalks. Parsley is always used fresh, never dried.

Mint is native to the Mediterranean too, and the variety most commonly grown and used is spearmint (*Mentha spicata*). It was grown by the Romans. Pliny claimed that if students wore a wreath of mint, it would 'exhilarate their mind'. Whether it is to stimulate the mind or to please the eye, mint is the favourite garnish in Lebanon and features on many mezze dishes. It is not wasted however, as diners often use the leaves to line their bread before scooping up hommus or kibbé.

Fresh mint also features in salads and dressings, while dried mint is added to yoghurt dishes and sauces.

Basil is not as widely used in mezze, but when it is, the choice is often the small leaf variety, commonly known as Greek basil. This is not to say that you cannot use the larger leaf basil that is more widely available here.

Purslane is still little known outside of the Mediterranean, even though it grows wild in many places. The leaf is fragile and bruises easily, which may explain why supermarkets so rarely stock it. Purslane is used in salads, as a filling for savoury pastries and, in Turkey, it is cooked like spinach.

The common cultivated variety of wild thyme (*Thymus vulgaris*) is used in its dried form in za'tar. To make this famous seasoning, mix 4 parts powdered dried thyme with 2 parts sumac, 1 part toasted sesame seeds and salt to taste.

A different, long thin-leaved variety of thyme (*Thymbra spicata*) is used fresh in mezze salads. It is available from Lebanese shops during the summer and early autumn.

As for dill, although it is also native to the eastern Mediterranean, it is not commonly used in Lebanon or Syria. However, it is the herb of choice in Greece and Turkey, where it is used fresh in dips and stuffed vegetables.

# fried aubergines with pomegranate dressing

*———— batinjan meqli*

Fried aubergines can be served in various ways: plain; with a yoghurt and garlic dip; topped with a spicy Lebanese tomato salsa (page 30); or as here, with a pomegranate syrup dressing – to me, the most interesting combination. The mild taste of velvety aubergines is deliciously offset by the sweet-sour syrup, mixed with garlic and good olive oil.

**serves 4–6**
4 medium aubergines, about 600g in total
salt
vegetable oil, for deep-frying

*for the pomegranate dressing*
2 tbsp pomegranate syrup
1 garlic clove, peeled and crushed
6 tbsp extra virgin olive oil
sea salt

Cut off the stem ends of the aubergines, then peel the skin away lengthways in strips to create a striped effect. Cut the aubergines lengthways into 1.5cm thick slices. Layer in a colander, sprinkling with salt, and leave to sweat for about 30 minutes. Rinse the slices under cold water and pat them dry with kitchen paper.

Pour a 4cm depth of vegetable oil into a large frying pan and place over a medium-high heat. To check that the oil is hot enough for deep-frying, dip in the tip of an aubergine slice; if the oil bubbles around it, it is ready. Slide in as many aubergine slices as will fit comfortably in the pan and fry until golden brown on both sides, about 5–6 minutes.

Carefully remove the fried aubergines with a slotted spoon and place on several layers of kitchen paper to drain off the excess oil. Cover with a double layer of kitchen paper and press lightly to soak up the oil from the surface. Repeat with the rest of the aubergines. Transfer to a flat serving platter.

For the pomegranate dressing, whisk the ingredients together in a bowl, adding 1 tbsp water and salt to taste. Drizzle the dressing over the aubergines. Serve at room temperature.

# courgettes in tomato sauce

*mûtabbaqat kûssa* ───────────────

This recipe belongs to the family of Lebanese dishes cooked in oil (*bil-zeyt*), which are staples of the mezze table. They are also served as main meals on Fridays and during Lent, when meat is off the menu. I like to use mini courgettes when they are available, but you can of course, simply use sliced courgettes, as indeed most Lebanese would.

**serves 4**
600g courgettes (preferably mini courgettes), trimmed
3 tbsp extra virgin olive oil
2 medium onions, peeled and thinly sliced
3 garlic cloves, peeled and thinly sliced
sea salt
2 x 400g cans cherry tomatoes, drained
1–1$\frac{1}{2}$ tbsp ground dried mint

If using the Middle Eastern variety of mini courgettes, cut in half lengthways; otherwise leave them whole. Cut regular courgettes on the slant into medium slices.

Heat the olive oil in a saucepan. Add the onions and garlic and fry over a medium heat, stirring occasionally, until lightly golden. Add the courgettes and a little salt and mix well. Lower the heat, cover and simmer for 5 minutes, stirring occasionally.

Add the tomatoes with a little more salt to taste. Increase the heat and bring to the boil, then re-cover the pan and boil over a medium-high heat for 15 minutes, stirring occasionally. If the sauce is boiling too hard, lower the heat slightly. Carefully stir in the mint and cook, uncovered, for another 5 minutes, or until the sauce has thickened.

Taste and adjust the seasoning, then remove from the heat and leave to cool. Serve at room temperature.

# fried cauliflower

*qarnabit meqli* ————

This is another typical Lebanese mezze. You can blanch the florets first if you like, but I prefer to fry them raw to retain a little crunch. Serve plain, with yoghurt, tahini dip (page 28), or even pomegranate dressing (page 108).

**serves 4–6**
2 medium cauliflowers
vegetable oil, for deep-frying
sea salt

Cut the cauliflowers into florets. Heat a 5cm depth of oil in a heavy-based pan over a medium heat. To check that the oil is hot, dip the bottom of a floret in; if the oil bubbles around it, then it is ready. Slide in as many florets as will fit comfortably in the pan and fry for about 6–8 minutes, turning them regularly until golden brown all over. Remove with a slotted spoon and drain on several layers of kitchen paper, while you fry the rest. Season with salt to taste. Serve warm or at room temperature.

# greek stuffed tomatoes

*domates yiemistes me ryzi* ————

**serves 4–6**
12 medium firm ripe tomatoes
75g short-grain rice, rinsed and drained
1 large onion, peeled and very finely chopped
3–4 tbsp finely chopped dill
2 tbsp finely chopped flat-leaf parsley
4 tbsp extra virgin olive oil
sea salt and freshly ground black pepper

These succulent tomatoes are usually served as a main course in Greece, but anything made small – or in smaller quantities – becomes a mezze.

Preheat the oven to 180°C/Gas 4. Slice the tops off the tomatoes and reserve. Scoop out the insides and chop finely. Put the rice in a bowl and add the chopped tomato pulp and juices, onion, herbs, 3 tbsp olive oil and salt and pepper to taste. Mix well.

Drizzle the remaining 1 tbsp oil in a baking dish that will hold the tomatoes snuggly. Fill the tomatoes with the stuffing, stand them in the baking dish and top with the reserved lids. Bake in the oven for about $1^1/_2$ hours until the rice is done. Serve warm or at room temperature.

# stuffed aubergines

*—— imam bayildi*

**serves 4–6**
12 small aubergines, about
  1kg in total
vegetable oil, for deep-frying

*for the stuffing*
2 medium tomatoes
3 tbsp extra virgin olive oil
4 medium onions, peeled
  and thinly sliced
6 garlic cloves, peeled and
  finely chopped
1 tsp tomato purée (paste)
2–3 flat-leaf parsley sprigs,
  stalk removed, finely
  chopped
sea salt

Cut off the stalk and hard skin around the top of the aubergines, then peel the skin away lengthways in broad strips to create a striped effect.

Heat a 4cm depth of vegetable oil in a large frying pan over a medium-high heat. To check that the oil is hot enough, dip the end of an aubergine into the oil; if the oil bubbles around it, it is ready. Drop in as many aubergines as will fit comfortably in the pan and fry for about 8–10 minutes until soft and golden brown all over, turning them over every now and then. Remove with a slotted spoon and place on several layers of kitchen paper to drain off the excess oil. Repeat with the rest of the aubergines.

To make the stuffing, halve and finely slice the tomatoes; set aside. Heat the olive oil in a large sauté pan. Add the onions and garlic and cook, stirring occasionally, until soft and transparent. Add the tomatoes and tomato purée and cook for a few minutes more. Stir in 150ml water and the chopped parsley and season with salt to taste. Simmer for 10 minutes.

Preheat the oven to 180°C/Gas 4. Slit each aubergine open lengthways to the middle, being careful not to cut right through to the other side. Carefully prise the aubergines open further and lay them in a shallow baking dish.

Spoon as much stuffing as you can inside each aubergine, piling a little more on top to form a shallow mound. Pour a little water into the dish to just cover the bottom and place in the oven. Bake in the oven for 30–40 minutes, or until the aubergines are soft.

Cover with a clean tea towel and let cool. You really need to handle the aubergines gently as they will be quite soft. Serve them at room temperature.

*Imam bayildi* is one of the great Turkish dishes. The name is almost always translated as 'the priest fainted', which is something of a mystery as it is difficult to believe any Turkish *Imam* would faint when given a dish comprising two of the most basic ingredients in Turkey. I use small aubergines here, but you can use larger ones if you like: simply halve four aubergines and fry before filling and baking, allowing a little longer in the oven.

# tomato 'burgers'
## —— *domatokeftethes*

**serves 4–6**

500g ripe tomatoes

2 medium onions, peeled
   and very finely chopped

30g mint sprigs, leaves
   only, finely chopped

few flat-leaf parsley sprigs,
   finely chopped

1 tbsp extra virgin olive oil,
   plus extra for shallow-
   frying

sea salt and freshly ground
   black pepper

150g self-raising flour

Here is the Greek version of the veggie burger. If you can't find good fresh tomatoes, use canned ones and drain them well, otherwise the mixture will be too wet. My friend and expert on Greek food, Aglaia Kremezi, uses ground *paximadi*, a Cretan rusk made partly with barley or wholewheat flour, instead of white flour. The resulting burgers have more texture.

Put the tomatoes in a large bowl and squeeze and crush them with your hands, until you have a tomato pulp. You need to use your hands rather than a food processor, otherwise the pulp will be lacking in texture and too watery.

Add the onions, herbs and 1 tbsp olive oil to the tomatoes, mix well and season with salt and pepper to taste. Add the flour and mix thoroughly until you have a thick, textured batter. Cover and let rest for 30 minutes.

Heat enough olive oil in a large frying pan over a medium heat to shallow-fry the tomato burgers. When the oil is hot, drop large tablespoonfuls of the tomato mixture into the pan, spacing them well apart, and spread into thin burgers. Fry for 3–4 minutes, or until golden underneath, then flip over and fry on the other side for 2–3 minutes more, or until crisp, golden and cooked through.

Transfer the burgers to a wire rack to keep them somewhat crisp while you fry the rest. Serve warm or at room temperature.

# stuffed vine leaves

*mehshi waraq 'enab bil-zeyt* ——

**serves 4**
200g preserved medium
  vine leaves (or fresh ones
  if you can find them)
1 large potato, peeled and
  sliced
1 large tomato, sliced
sea salt

*for the filling*
150g short-grain white rice,
  rinsed and drained
300g firm red tomatoes,
  finely diced
50g spring onions, trimmed
  and thinly sliced
100g flat-leaf parsley, most
  of the stalk discarded,
  chopped medium-fine
50g mint, leaves only,
  chopped medium-fine
2 heaped tbsp sumac
$1/4$ tsp ground cinnamon
$1/2$ tsp Lebanese 7-spice
  mixture (or ground
  allspice)
$1/4$ tsp finely ground black
  pepper
juice of 1 large lemon, or
  to taste
150ml extra virgin olive oil

*to serve*
thin lemon wedges

Stuffing vine leaves is time-consuming, though quicker with practice. Lebanese chefs have a way of bunching up the leaf around the filling and rolling it in seconds. Fortunately, you can prepare them a day ahead – they taste even better the next day. And you can use this stuffing to fill blanched Swiss Chard leaves, or small peppers or tomatoes.

To make the filling, mix all the ingredients together in a bowl, seasoning with salt to taste. It should look like a salad.

Take a vine leaf, cut away the stem, if any, and lay flat on a surface, smooth side down and stem end towards you. Spoon $1/2$–$1 1/2$ tsp stuffing (depending on size of leaf) in a thin line across the leaf, about 1.5cm from the tip of the stem and the same distance short of the sides. (The line should be thinner than your little finger.) Fold the sides over the rice, tapering slightly towards the bottom. Then fold the top edge over the stuffing and roll neatly but loosely – to leave space for the rice to expand during cooking.

Line the bottom of a saucepan with the potato and tomato slices. Place the rolled vine leaf, loose end down, on the tomatoes. Continue filling, rolling and arranging the vine leaves, side by side in the pan, one layer at a time until you've finished.

Swirl some water around the empty stuffing bowl to extract the last bits of flavouring, pour over the leaves to barely cover them and add salt. Place an upturned heatproof plate over the stuffed leaves to stop them from unravelling and put the lid on. Bring to the boil, then lower the heat and simmer for 1 hour, or until done – taste one to make sure the rice is cooked.

Let cool in the pan, then carefully transfer the stuffed leaves to a platter. Serve at room temperature, with lemon wedges.

# spicy fried potatoes

*———— batata harrah*

Flavouring fried potatoes with garlic, chilli and fresh coriander is a great way to lift them. Usually they are fried in cubes, but I prefer to use new potatoes, which I cut into small wedges, or if I can find really small new potatoes, I fry them whole. Some Arab chefs add chopped onion and peppers to the coriander and garlic mixture, but I like the simplicity of this seasoning. The potatoes stay crisp and the taste is sharp and clean.

Cut the potatoes into wedges. Heat a 5cm depth of oil in a heavy-based wide pan over a medium heat. To check that the oil is hot, dip a potato piece in the oil; if the oil bubbles around the potato, it is ready. Drop in as many potato wedges as will fit comfortably in the pan. Fry for about 8 minutes, turning them every now and then, until the potatoes are crisp and golden brown all over.

Remove with a slotted spoon on to several layers of kitchen paper to drain off the excess oil. Fry the rest of the potatoes and drain in the same way. Season with salt and set aside.

Melt the butter in a large frying pan over a medium-high heat. Add the coriander, garlic and chilli flakes and stir until the aroma rises. Add the fried potato wedges and sauté for a couple of minutes until the potatoes are coated with the mixture. Taste and adjust the seasoning if necessary. Serve immediately.

**serves 6**

1kg medium new potatoes, scrubbed clean

vegetable oil, for deep-frying

sea salt

30g unsalted butter

200g coriander sprigs, most of the stalk removed, chopped medium-fine

4 garlic cloves, peeled and crushed

1/4 tsp dried chilli flakes

fish & shellfish

# turkish
# **mussel** brochettes
—— *midye tava*

**serves 4–6**
40 large mussels, shelled
  (defrosted if frozen)

*for the batter*
225g organic (unbleached)
  plain flour
45g cornflour
1½ tsp bicarbonate of soda
1 tbsp sea salt
330ml sparkling water

*to cook and serve*
sunflower oil, for deep-
  frying
lemon wedges

These brochettes are typical street food in Turkey. The mussels are usually slipped off their skewers into a fat baguette and drizzled with a thinner version of walnut tarator (page 36). The best type to use are the large New Zealand green-lip mussels, which are generally sold frozen. If you are able to buy large fresh mussels, steam them open and shell them first. If you don't have a big enough pan to fry the mussels on skewers, simply dip them individually in batter and deep-fry.

First make the batter. Mix the dry ingredients together in a bowl, then slowly whisk in the sparkling water to make a smooth batter. Cover and set aside.

For the skewers, you'll need about 24 short wooden skewers. Thread 3 or 4 mussels on to each pair of skewers (as shown). Heat a 4cm depth of sunflower oil in a large, deep, heavy-based sauté or frying pan over a medium-high heat to deep-fry the mussels. To check that the oil is ready, dip a piece of bread into it; if the oil bubbles around the bread, it is ready.

Dip a skewer in the batter, remove and slide it into the hot oil. Add as many battered skewers as will fit comfortably in the pan and deep-fry for 30 seconds or so on each side, or until golden all over.

Carefully remove the mussel skewers as soon as they are done and place on several layers of kitchen paper to drain off the excess oil and keep the mussels crisp. Deep-fry the rest of the brochettes in the same way, skimming the oil clean in between each batch so that you don't end up with burnt bits of batter clinging to the mussels.

Sprinkle the fried mussels with a little salt. Serve immediately, with lemon wedges, and walnut tarator if you like.

# greek octopus salad

———— *htapothi vrasto*

Not so long ago my fishmonger sent me small squid by mistake when I asked him for baby octopus. I used the squid to make this salad, but it was not as pretty, nor as tasty. Surprisingly, the texture was different too. If you can't find baby octopus, buy full-grown instead, simmer until tender, then slice thinly on the slant. This is how it is served in Greece. Again, it won't be as gorgeous as the one opposite, but it will taste good all the same.

**serves 4–6**
1 lemon, halved
1kg baby octopus
sea salt

*for the dressing*
4 tbsp extra virgin olive oil
juice of $\frac{1}{2}$ lemon, or to taste
$\frac{3}{4}$ tsp dried oregano
freshly ground black pepper

Bring a pot full of water to the boil, then reduce the heat to low, add the lemon halves and wait until the water is at a bare simmer. Add the baby octopus and some salt and simmer for 10–15 minutes until tender.

Meanwhile, for the dressing, whisk the ingredients together in a large bowl. When the octopus is done, drain it well in a colander. Add to the dressing and toss well, then taste and adjust the seasoning if necessary. Serve warm, at room temperature or slightly chilled.

# fried **whitebait**

——— *samak bizreh*

This is one of the most common mezze in Turkey, Greece and Lebanon. You can vary the whitebait by frying calamari rings, baby octopus or tiny transparent fish. These 'glass fish' as I call them are not easy to find, but they are definitely worth buying if your fishmonger has them. As they fry, the little fish clump together to make totally scrumptious fritters.

**serves 4–6**
1kg whitebait
flour, for coating
sea salt and freshly ground
  black pepper
vegetable oil, for deep-
  frying

*to serve*
tahini dip (page 28)
lemon wedges

Gently rinse and drain the fish. Put enough flour to coat the fish in a large plastic bag (ideally a zip-lock one). Add salt and pepper, close the bag and shake to mix. Then add the fish, close the bag again and shake to coat the fish with seasoned flour. Put a large, dry colander in the sink and empty the contents of the bag into it. Shake gently from side to side to get rid of any excess flour.

Heat the vegetable oil in a suitable pan for deep-frying over a medium heat. To check that the oil is hot enough, dip a piece of bread in; if the oil bubbles around the bread, it is ready. Drop in as much fish as will fit comfortably in the pan. Deep-fry, turning to colour the fish evenly, for 2–4 minutes until they are crisp and golden.

Remove the fish with a slotted spoon and scatter over several layers of kitchen paper to drain off the excess oil. Sprinkle with more salt if necessary. Fry the remaining fish in the same way.

Serve immediately, while crisp and hot, with the tahini dip and lemon wedges.

# turkish
# mussel 'rısotto'

*midye pilavi* ————

**serves 4–6**

1.5kg fresh mussels

250g Calasparra or Bomba rice

100ml extra virgin olive oil

2 medium onions, peeled and finely chopped

2 tbsp pine nuts

2 tbsp sultanas

3 tbsp tomato purée (paste)

1/2 tsp ground cinnamon

1/2 tsp ground allspice

1/2 tsp sweet paprika

1/4 tsp cayenne pepper

1/4 tsp ground cloves

sea salt and freshly ground black pepper

2 tbsp chopped flat-leaf parsley

2 tbsp chopped dill

lemon wedges, to serve

In Turkey, stuffed mussels are sold as street food, which is rather puzzling as they are quite time-consuming. I love them, but I don't relish the idea of spending hours cutting raw mussels open and stuffing them, so I bring the ingredients together in a different way – to produce an exotic and delectable 'risotto'.

Scrub the mussels thoroughly under cold running water and discard any that are open and do not close when tapped sharply with the back of a knife. Put the rice in a bowl, add warm water to cover and set aside to soak.

Heat the olive oil in a saucepan over a medium heat, add the onions and pine nuts and cook, stirring occasionally, until lightly golden. Drain the rice and add to the pan. Sauté for a minute or so, then add the sultanas, tomato purée, spices and seasoning. Pour in 500ml water, bring to the boil and then lower the heat. Cover and simmer, stirring every now and then, for 10 minutes, or until the rice is just done and still slightly moist.

Take the pan off the heat, add the chopped herbs and fork through the rice. Wrap the lid with a tea towel and replace on the pan. Let stand until the rice is just warm.

In the meantime, put the mussels in a large saucepan (with a tight-fitting lid). Add enough water to cover the bottom of the pan by about 2cm and place over a high heat. Bring to the boil and cook for 2–4 minutes, shaking the pan every now and then, until the mussels open – do not overcook them or they will shrink and become rubbery. Drain the mussels and shell them, discarding any unopened ones.

Add the mussels to the warm rice and toss well. Taste and adjust the seasoning if necessary. Serve warm or at room temperature, with lemon wedges.

# sardines wrapped in vine leaves

*sardalya sarmasi*

There is a very short time during the year, in late spring/ early summer, when you can buy vine leaves fresh from Middle Eastern shops. Or, if you are lucky enough to have a grapevine growing in your garden, you can pick your own. If you are using fresh leaves, you will need to blanch them first, otherwise follow the instructions below for the preserved leaves.

### serves 4–6
12 fresh sardines, 80–90g each, gutted
sea salt and freshly ground black pepper
12 preserved vine leaves, rinsed, stalks removed

Preheat the oven to 220°C/Gas 7. Rinse the sardines under cold running water and lay them on a platter. Season with salt and pepper – salt sparingly if you are wrapping them in preserved vine leaves as these will still be somewhat salty after rinsing.

Lay one vine leaf on a board, glossy side down, and place a sardine in the centre. Wrap the leaf around the fish, tucking one end under it and folding the other end in, so that it doesn't wrap over. Place on a non-stick baking sheet, loose side down. Wrap the other sardines in the same way and place them on the baking sheet.

Bake in the oven for 15 minutes until the sardines are just done and the leaves are crisp on the edges. Serve immediately, or let them cool for a while to serve warm or at room temperature.

# lebanese **fish kibbé**

—— *kibbet samak*

**serves 4–6**
olive oil, to oil dish

*for the filling*
250g onions, peeled and
 thinly sliced
60g pine nuts
75ml extra virgin olive oil
1/4 tsp finely ground white
 pepper
sea salt

*for the kibbé*
100g coriander sprigs,
 most of the stalk removed
600g red bream fillets,
 skinned
1 medium onion, peeled
 and quartered
grated zest of 1/2 orange
 or lemon (preferably
 unwaxed)
150g fine burghul, rinsed
 and drained
1/2 tsp ground cinnamon
1/4 tsp finely ground white
 pepper

Fish kibbé isn't normally part of a mezze but I find that it adds a light, yet substantial note to a mezze served as a meal. Here I make one large cake, but you can shape small ones, using individual pie dishes if you prefer.

Preheat the oven to 200°C/Gas 6. Oil a round baking dish, about 29cm in diameter, with a little olive oil.

For the filling, put the sliced onions, pine nuts and olive oil in a bowl. Season with the pepper and salt and mix well. Set aside.

For the kibbé, put the coriander in a food processor, together with the fish, onion and orange zest. Process until quite smooth, then transfer to a bowl. Add the burghul, cinnamon, pepper and salt to taste. Mix with your hand until evenly combined.

Have a bowl of lightly salted water to hand as you shape the fish cake. Divide the kibbé in half and set aside one half (for the top). Moisten your hands with water and pinch off a handful of kibbé from the other portion. Flatten between your palms to a 1cm thickness and place in the baking dish, next to one edge. Smooth it down evenly with your fingers.

Pinch off more kibbé, flatten and lay next to the first piece, slightly overlapping it. Dip your fingers in water and smooth the pieces together until the join disappears. Continue until you've covered the bottom of the dish, then moisten your fingers again and smooth into an even layer.

Spread the stuffing evenly over the kibbé and cover with the remaining fish mixture, following the same method as before (it will be slightly more difficult to spread).

Cut the pie into quarters, then mark a pattern across the top of each quarter with a knife for a decorative finish, if you like. Make a hole in the centre with your finger and, finally, drizzle olive oil all over the top of the kibbé. Bake for 15 minutes, or until cooked to your liking. Serve hot, warm or at room temperature.

# sardines chermûla

———— *hût bil chermûla*

**serves 4–6**
8 sardines, boned and
  butterflied (see note)

*for the chermûla*
3 garlic cloves, peeled and
  crushed
1 small onion, peeled and
  very finely chopped
100g coriander sprigs,
  most of the stalk removed,
  very finely chopped
1 tsp ground cumin
1/2 tsp paprika
1/4 tsp crushed dried chillies
4 tbsp extra virgin olive oil
juice of 1 1/2 lemons, or
  to taste
sea salt

*to finish*
vegetable oil, for frying
flour, for coating

Butterflied sardines, sandwiched together in pairs with a little chermûla and deep-fried, are typical street food in Morocco. I prepare mine a little differently – keeping them single and shallow-frying them. Sometimes I turn the marinade into a batter and make chermûla fritters to serve alongside the sardines (see below). If you can't find fresh sardines, use thin white fish fillets instead.

Rinse the butterflied sardines and pat them dry. Mix the chermûla ingredients together in a large bowl. Add the sardines and carefully turn to coat them. Leave to marinate in a cool place for at least 2 hours.

Heat a 2cm layer of vegetable oil in a deep frying pan over a medium-high heat. When the oil is hot, take the sardines one at a time from the chermûla, drain well and dip into the flour, then slip into the hot pan, skin side down. Repeat with as many sardines as will fit comfortably in the pan. Fry for 1–2 minutes on each side until golden. Remove with a slotted spoon and place on several layers of kitchen paper to drain off excess oil and keep crisp, while you cook the rest. Serve hot or warm.

**note**  If possible, get your fishmonger to butterfly the sardines, otherwise you'll need to do this yourself. First cut the head off, then slit the belly open all the way down to the tail. Remove the innards, then slide your thumb under the backbone to loosen it. Slide your index finger under the other side and lift the bone up. You can, at this stage, cut the tail off with the bone but I like to keep it on and just cut the bone where it joins the tail.

**chermûla fritters**  Mix 1 egg, 150g plain flour, 1/2 tsp easy-blend dried yeast and 160ml water into the marinade after removing the sardines. Let rest for 40 minutes. To cook, heat a thin film of olive oil in a large frying pan, drop in large spoonfuls of the batter and fry, turning once, until golden on both sides.

# calamari in tomato sauce

*kalamarakia me domathes*

Here is a simple Greek mezze that you can vary by replacing the tomatoes with squid ink (as below). This is available in sachets from good fishmongers and delicatessens.

## serves 4–6

1kg baby squid (calamari), cleaned

3 tbsp extra virgin olive oil

1 medium onion, peeled and finely chopped

2 garlic cloves, peeled and finely chopped

2 x 400g cans cherry tomatoes, drained

1 tsp dried oregano

1 tsp Aleppo pepper

sea salt and freshly ground black pepper

few flat-leaf parsley sprigs, most of the stalk removed, finely chopped

Rinse the baby squid under cold running water and peel off the membrane if necessary. Set aside to drain.

Heat the olive oil in a large sauté pan over a medium heat. Add the onion and cook, stirring regularly, until soft and translucent. Add the garlic and continue cooking for a minute or so, until lightly golden.

Add the squid to the pan and increase the heat to medium high. Cook, stirring every now and then, until nearly all the liquid from the squid has evaporated. This will take about 15 minutes, as they release an astonishing amount of juice.

Add the tomatoes, oregano, Aleppo pepper and salt and pepper to taste. Lower the heat to medium, cover the pan and cook for 10 minutes, stirring the squid every now and then. Reduce the heat to low and simmer for another 10 minutes, or until the squid is done and the sauce is well reduced.

Stir in the chopped parsley and remove from the heat. Taste and adjust the seasoning if necessary. Cover the pan with a tea towel and let cool slightly. Serve warm or at room temperature.

## variation

**calamari in squid ink** Omit the tomatoes. Increase the olive oil to 4 tbsp and use 3 medium onions. After sautéeing the onion, pour in 3 sachets squid ink and 250ml water. Add the squid and continue as above.

# fish in tahini sauce

*——— tajen samak*

I usually prepare this dish with black cod, a rather unorthodox, extravagant fish to use here, but it works well with the sauce and it is one of my favourite fish. However, you can use any firm-textured white variety. The fish is typically stewed in the tahini sauce, but I prefer to cook it separately and slip it into the sauce at the last minute so it doesn't overcook.

Mix the tahini with the crushed garlic in a bowl. Slowly add the lemon juice, stirring as you do so – at first the tahini will thicken, then it will thin out again as you add more liquid. Gradually add 200ml water, still stirring, until you have a thin creamy sauce. Season with salt to taste. Set aside.

Heat 1 tbsp olive oil in a non-stick frying pan over a medium-high heat. When it is hot, slide the fish fillets in, skin side down, and cook for about 2 minutes until the skin is crisp and golden. Turn the fillets over and cook for another minute or so, until the fish is just done. Carefully transfer to a plate.

Add the remaining 3 tbsp olive oil to the pan. Add the onions and cook, stirring occasionally, until soft and lightly golden. Add the tahini sauce and cumin and season with salt and white pepper to taste. Mix well, then let bubble for 3–4 minutes, stirring every now and then, until the tahini just starts to separate and you see a little oil coming to the surface.

Take the pan off the heat and slide the fish into the sauce. Scatter the pine nuts all over. Gently shake the pan back and forth to coat the fish with the sauce. Taste and adjust the seasoning if necessary. Serve warm.

**serves 4–6**
125ml tahini
2 garlic cloves, peeled and crushed
juice of 1½ lemons, or to taste
sea salt
4 tbsp extra virgin olive oil
450g white fish fillet (sea bass, bream or similar), cut into portions
3 medium onions, peeled and thinly sliced
1 tsp ground cumin
freshly ground white pepper
2 tbsp pine nuts, toasted

# chicken wings,
# kibbé & other meat

# barbecued
# chicken wings
—— *jawaneh*

**serves 4–6**
800g small chicken wings,
  tip removed and cut in two

*for the marinade*
4 large garlic cloves, peeled
  and crushed
1 tbsp extra virgin olive oil
juice of ½ lemon, or to
  taste
pinch of ground cinnamon
¼ tsp Lebanese 7-spice
  mixture (or ground
  allspice)
pinch of cayenne pepper
sea salt
¼ tsp freshly ground black
  pepper

*for the aïoli*
2 egg yolks
1 garlic clove, peeled and
  crushed
sea salt
4–6 tbsp extra virgin olive
  oil
juice of ½ lemon, or to
  taste

Small chicken wings are perfect for this recipe. My butcher removes the tip from small wings and cuts them in two – to produce a fleshy mini drumstick-like part and a crisp, juicy flat part. I generally roast mine in the oven but they are really best cooked over a charcoal fire, or grilled. You can use drumsticks in place of the wings if you like – buy 8–12 depending on how many you are serving.

Mix the marinade ingredients together in a large bowl. Add the chicken wings and toss to coat well. Leave to marinate for at least 30 minutes, preferably 2 hours, turning the wings regularly.

In the meantime, make the aïoli. Whisk the egg yolks, crushed garlic and a little salt together in a bowl. Then, slowly drizzle in the olive oil, whisking all the time, until you have a thick aïoli. Stir in the lemon juice. Taste and adjust the seasoning if necessary and add a little more olive oil if the aïoli is too runny.

Preheat the oven to 200°C/Gas 6, or your grill to maximum, or heat up a charcoal barbecue. Roast the wings in the oven for 30 minutes, or until crisp on the outside and tender but fully cooked inside. If you are grilling or barbecuing the wings, cook them for at least 10 minutes on each side, or until the skin is slightly charred and the meat is cooked through.

Serve the chicken wings immediately, with the aïoli.

# circassian chicken

——— *çerkez tavugu*

**serves 4–6**
1 organic chicken, about 1.5kg
1 onion, peeled and spiked with 3 cloves
1 carrot, peeled and halved
1 celery stick, halved
1 leek, washed and halved
few flat-leaf parsley sprigs
sea salt

*for the sauce*
125g shelled walnuts
1 garlic clove, peeled
50g fresh breadcrumbs
2 tsp Aleppo pepper

*to assemble*
50g unsalted butter
1 small onion, peeled and very finely chopped

*to serve*
4 tbsp walnut oil
1 tsp paprika

This is a classic Turkish mezze, which can be served warm or at room temperature. Poached chicken is dressed in a subtly spiced walnut and garlic sauce – a great way to pep it up. I like to season the sauce with mildly spicy Aleppo pepper, which is more or less the same as *pul biber*. You can use a mix of 1 tsp paprika and 1 tsp cayenne pepper instead if you prefer, though the dish will lose its lovely bright red chilli flecks.

Put the chicken into a large pan with the onion, carrot, celery, leek and parsley. Pour in enough water to barely cover and place over a medium-high heat. As the water is about to come to the boil, skim the surface. Then add salt to taste, cover the pan, lower the heat and simmer for 45 minutes, or until the chicken is done. Lift it out on to a board and remove the skin and bones. Shred the meat and place in a bowl. Cover and set aside. Strain the stock and reserve.

To make the sauce, put the walnuts, garlic, breadcrumbs, pepper and 200ml of the reserved stock in a food processor. Whiz until you have a very fine-textured sauce. Set aside.

Melt the butter in a large frying pan. Add the onion and cook over a medium-high heat, stirring regularly, until soft and lightly golden. Add the chicken and 200ml of the reserved stock. Let bubble gently for about 10 minutes until most of the liquor has evaporated. Add the walnut sauce to the chicken and stir well. Cover the pan with a clean tea towel and let cool until warm or at room temperature.

When ready to serve, flavour the walnut oil with the paprika. Transfer the chicken and sauce to a serving dish. Drizzle the flavoured oil over the chicken and sprinkle with a little more pepper if you like. Serve immediately.

# sautéed **chicken livers**

*qasbet djaj meqliyeh* ——

**serves 4**
3 tbsp extra virgin olive oil
1 medium onion, peeled
   and spiked with 5 cloves
500g organic chicken
   livers, trimmed
1/2 tsp Lebanese 7-spice
   mixture (or ground
   allspice)
1/4 tsp finely ground black
   pepper
sea salt
3 garlic cloves, peeled and
   crushed
juice of 1 lemon, or to taste
1 tbsp finely chopped
   coriander

Sautéed chicken livers are an essential part of a Lebanese mezze. Adding the garlic, lemon juice and coriander at the end gives a lovely fresh touch. Make sure you have these ingredients prepared and ready to hand before you start sautéeing the livers, as you don't want to overcook them.

Put the olive oil and onion in a large frying pan over a medium-high heat. When hot, add the chicken livers and fry them for 2 minutes. Turn the livers over and cook for a further 1 minute.

Season with the spice mix or allspice, pepper and salt to taste. Add the garlic and lemon juice and toss well, then scatter over the chopped coriander.

Serve immediately, or at least while still warm.

# grilled spiced quail

*firreh mishweh* ——————————

Quail can be prepared in various ways for grilling or roasting – by cutting down the back to butterfly them, by simply cutting in half, or they can be left whole if you like. I usually roast the birds in the oven, but I have to admit they taste even better when they're cooked over a charcoal fire.

**serves 4–6**
6 quails

*for the marinade*
4 large garlic cloves, peeled and crushed
1 tbsp extra virgin olive oil
juice of $1/2$ lemon, or to taste
pinch of ground cinnamon
$1/4$ tsp Lebanese 7-spice mixture (or ground allspice)
pinch of cayenne pepper
sea salt
$1/4$ tsp freshly ground black pepper

To butterfly the quails, cut the back in half using poultry shears, then turn the birds over and press on the breast to flatten them. (Or to halve them, cut the back as above, then turn the birds and cut down the breast bone to divide into two neat halves.) Trim any unsightly bones.

Mix the marinade ingredients together in a large bowl. Add the quails and turn to coat. Marinate for at least 30 minutes, ideally $1 1/2$–2 hours, turning them every now and then.

Preheat the oven to 200°C/Gas 6, or your grill to maximum, or heat up the barbecue. Roast the birds in the oven for 30 minutes, or until golden and cooked through. Or grill or barbecue the quails for 10–15 minutes on each side until completely done. Serve immediately.

# marinated lamb cutlets

—— *kastalettah meshwiyeh*

**serves 4–6**
12 lamb cutlets

*for the marinade*
2 tbsp extra virgin olive oil
1 garlic clove, peeled and
  crushed
1 tbsp dried oregano
juice of ¹/₂ lemon, or to
  taste
sea salt and freshly ground
  black pepper

Lamb chops are not exactly mezze fare, not even in Greece where this marinade comes from. They usually follow after, along with other grilled meats, but I like to include them in the spread, especially if I'm serving mezze as a full meal. Cutlets are small and dainty enough to be picked up by hand and nibbled on. They will also add meatiness to a spread that is otherwise largely vegetarian.

Mix the marinade ingredients together in a large bowl, adding salt and pepper to taste. Add the lamb cutlets and toss to coat. Cover and leave to marinate for at least 30 minutes, preferably overnight in the fridge.

Preheat the grill to maximum, or heat up a charcoal barbecue (this being the most delicious way to cook the meat). Grill or barbecue the chops for 2–5 minutes on each side, depending on how well done you like your meat. Serve hot or warm.

# spiced herby meat balls

*kefta* ———————

The spicing for these Lebanese meat balls is fairly simple, but I've also given a Moroccan variation, which has a more complex flavouring. Both are delicious and easy to make. *Kefta* is traditionally wrapped around skewers and grilled over charcoal, but I shape mine into balls and either bake or sauté them.

Put the onions and parsley in a food processor and pulse to chop coarsely. Add the lamb and process until the meat is finely ground. Transfer to a bowl and add the spices, pepper and salt to taste. Mix with your hands until evenly blended.

To shape each kefta ball, pinch off a little meat and roll between the palms of your hands to a ball, the size of a walnut. If you are sautéeing the kefta, I suggest you chill them for 30 minutes, so that they firm up and do not lose their shape.

If baking, preheat the oven to 230°C/Gas 8. Place the kefta balls on a non-stick baking sheet and bake for 10 minutes, or until done to your liking.

To sauté, heat a little oil in a sauté pan over a medium-high heat. Sauté the kefta balls in batches for 2–3 minutes, or until golden brown all over. Using a slotted spoon, transfer to several layers of kitchen paper to drain while you cook the rest.

Serve the kefta hot, warm or at room temperature, with pickles (see overleaf) and/or Lebanese tomato salsa (page 30).

**makes 28–30 balls**

2 medium onions, peeled and quartered
100g flat-leaf parsley, most of the stalk discarded
600g boneless leg of lamb, skinned, trimmed of fat and minced
$1/2$ tsp ground cinnamon
$1/2$ tsp Lebanese 7-spice mixture (or ground allspice)
$1/4$ tsp finely ground black pepper
sea salt
vegetable oil, for shallow-frying (optional)

## variation

**morrocan kefta**  Use 600g lamb, as above, and flavour with 1 small onion, 30g fresh coriander, 30g flat-leaf parsley, 2 mint sprigs (leaves only), $1/2$ tsp each ground cumin and paprika, $1/4$ tsp each ground allspice, dried chilli flakes and *ras el hanout* (Moroccan spice mix), plus sea salt.

# pickles

Pickles, like nuts, olives and bread, are an essential part of the mezze table. In homes, you will usually be offered a few pickles, while in restaurants a bigger selection is served.

As a child, I loved to watch my mother prepare pickles. The kitchen counters were covered with glass jars and mounds of vegetables. Depending on the season, she pickled cucumbers, turnips (with pieces of beetroot to colour them pink), peppers stuffed with cabbage, and aubergines. She would prepare them at the height of the season when the vegetable was at its best and cheapest, and there was always enough to last the whole year.

The Lebanese pickling solution is made up of 1 part vinegar to 2 or 3 parts water. The salt is calculated at 10 per cent of the amount of water and the sugar at 1.5 per cent. Pink pickled turnips (coloured with beetroot), cucumbers and peppers are especially popular.

However, the country that is most famous for its pickles is Turkey. There you will find specialist pickle shops that sell nothing but pickles. Old-fashioned shops have huge barrels of pickles (the shopkeeper scoops out as much you require) while modern shops have neat displays of pickles packed in glass jars. Turks seem to pickle everything. The choice of vegetables includes string beans, carrots, green tomatoes, beetroot, garlic, okra, aubergines stuffed with shredded cabbage, cauliflower and red cabbage. You can also buy pickled herbs such as dill, or pickled eggs. And there is a huge array of pickled fruit, such as plums, unripe melons, medlars, cherries, apples, quince, sour cherries, apricots, peaches and pears. The list is endless...

The pickling solution in Turkey is generally made of grape vinegar (no alcohol as it is a Muslim country), lemon juice, water and salt. Of course, this solution varies from region to another, even from family to family.

In Turkey, you will come across ambulant vendors pushing pickle carts along the streets. Once you've chosen your pickles to snack on, the vendor will usually offer you some pickling solution to drink. It is surprisingly pleasant and refreshing!

Neither the Moroccans nor the Greeks have as extensive a repertoire of pickles as the Lebanese or Turks. In Morocco, lemons are preserved in salt or in brine, while in Greece pickled olives are most common. Greeks also pickle cooked octopus, which is preserved in vinegar.

The name for pickles in Turkish is *tursu*, while in Arabic several names are used: *kabiss*, *mûkhallal* and *torshi*.

# kibbé balls
—— *kibbeh qrass*

**makes 20 balls**

*for the stuffing*

90g unsalted butter

60g pine nuts

500g large onions, peeled and finely chopped

200g finely minced lamb (from the leanest part of the leg)

2 tsp ground cinnamon

2 tsp Lebanese 7-spice mixture (or ground allspice)

1/2 tsp finely ground black pepper

sea salt

*for the kibbé*

200g fine burghul

1 medium onion, peeled and quartered

500g finely minced lamb (from the leanest part of the leg)

2 tsp ground cinnamon

2 tsp Lebanese 7-spice mixture (or ground allspice)

1/2 tsp finely ground black pepper

melted butter, for brushing

This is probably the most intricate recipe in the book, but kibbé balls are an important part of a Lebanese mezze and you will soon get the hang of making them! If possible, get your butcher to mince the lamb for you. And be sure to use very fine burghul, otherwise the mixture will be too coarse and tricky to shape. Kibbé balls are normally fried, but I prefer to bake them.

For the stuffing, melt the butter in a deep frying pan and sauté the pine nuts over a medium heat until golden brown. Remove with a slotted spoon and set aside. Fry the chopped onions in the same pan until soft and transparent. Add the minced lamb and cook until it loses all traces of pink, mashing and stirring with a spoon or fork so that it does not form lumps. Take off the heat and season with the cinnamon, spice mix, pepper and salt to taste. Stir in the pine nuts. Set aside.

For the kibbé, wash the burghul in several changes of cold water, then drain well. Put the onion in a food processor and pulse until finely chopped, then add the meat and process until well combined. Add the burghul and pulse a few times to mix. Transfer the mixture to a bowl and add the cinnamon, spice mix or allspice, pepper and salt to taste.

Have a bowl of lightly salted water to hand. Mix the kibbé until the spices are well incorporated, using your hand and dipping it every now and then into salted water to moisten. Knead the meat mixture for about 3 minutes until you have a smooth paste. Taste and adjust the seasoning if necessary.

Divide the kibbé into 20 balls, each the size of a large plum. Shape and fill, according to the instructions overleaf. (If you have any stuffing left, fry some eggs on it.)

Preheat the oven to 180°C/Gas 4. Brush the kibbé balls with melted butter and bake for 20–25 minutes, or until crisp and lightly golden. Serve hot, warm or at room temperature.

chicken wings, kibbé & other meat

### shaping a kibbé ball

Lightly moisten your hands and place a meat ball in the cup of one hand. With the index finger of your other hand burrow a hole into the meat ball while rotating it – to make the hollowing out easier and more even. You should end up with a thin shell resembling a topless egg; take care to avoid piercing it.

Spoon 1 1/2–2 tsp stuffing into the meat shell, gently pushing it in carefully with your fingers. Pinch the open edges together, then cup your free fingers over the top and gently shape into an ovoid ball with slightly pointed ends. Place on a non-stick baking sheet.

# turkish kibbé

—— *çig köfte*

This is the spicy Turkish take on Lebanese raw kibbé (recipe opposite). In Turkey, *çig köfte* is sold on the street, wheeled around in carts or carried on trays to be sold wrapped in flat bread with salad as a sandwich, or hawked to diners in open-air restaurants for them to add to their mezze. The Turkish version has more burghul and more spices and flavourings added to the meat, so the taste and texture are significantly different.

Put the spring onions and garlic in the food processor and whiz until very finely chopped. Add the parsley and process until medium-fine. Transfer to a bowl. Add the minced meat, tomato purée, chilli flakes, ground spices and salt and pepper.

Rinse the burghul in several changes of cold water. Drain thoroughly and add to the meat mixture.

Have a bowl of lightly salted cold water to hand. Mix the kibbé ingredients together with your hand until well blended, dipping your hand in the water every now and then.

Lightly wet both hands and shape the mixture into 12 torpedos. Squeeze gently on each to make indentations with your fingers. Arrange in a circle on a serving platter and pile the mint leaves into the centre. Serve immediately.

**serves 4**
4 spring onions, trimmed
1 garlic clove, peeled
50g coarsely chopped flat-leaf parsley
150g very fresh finely minced lamb (from the leanest part of the leg)
1½ tsp tomato purée (paste)
1 tsp dried chilli flakes, or to taste
⅛ tsp ground ginger
¼ tsp ground cloves
¼ tsp ground cumin
¼ tsp ground cinnamon
¼ tsp ground allspice
sea salt and freshly ground black pepper
100g fine burghul
handful of mint leaves, for garnish

# nayla's herb kibbé

*fraket nayla* ————

I have my friend, Nayla Audi, to thank for this recipe. Sunday lunches at her family's home in Kfar Rumman in southern Lebanon are wonderful, with the whole family gathered around a mezze of different kibbés, this one included. If you prefer, you can spread the herby burghul mix over the raw meat to eat them together, rather than mixed. The taste is quite different.

**serves 4–6**

1 small onion, peeled and quartered
50g flat-leaf parsley, most of the stalk removed
30g marjoram or oregano sprigs, leaves only
small handful of basil leaves, plus extra for garnish
2 dried rosebuds
finely grated zest of $1/2$ unwaxed lemon
finely grated zest of $1/2$ unwaxed orange
100g fine burghul
sea salt and freshly ground black pepper
300g very fresh finely minced lamb (from the leanest part of the leg)
extra virgin olive oil, for drizzling

Put the onion, herbs and rosebuds in a food processor and process until very fine. Transfer to a large bowl and add the citrus zests and burghul. Season with salt and pepper to taste and mix well.

Have a bowl of lightly salted cold water to hand. Add the minced lamb to the herb mixture and mix well with your hand, dipping it in the water every now and then. Divide the meat into 12 pieces and shape each into a torpedo. Squeeze it slightly to make indentations with your fingers.

Arrange the kibbé in a circle on a serving platter and pile basil leaves into the centre. Serve immediately, with olive oil for those who would like to drizzle some over their kibbé.

# quail's eggs
## with spicy sausage

*beyd firreh meqli ala sujuk*

This recipe is usually made by frying regular hen's eggs in the pan with the sausage. It is delicious but not as pretty as tiny fried quail's egg served on pan-fried slices of *sujuk*. The taste is also cleaner and more refined.

Brush a large non-stick frying pan with olive oil and place over a medium-high heat. When hot, very carefully break 3 or 4 quail's eggs into the pan. Fry for a couple of minutes, or until the white is just set. Remove to a plate and keep warm while you cook the rest.

Put as many sausage slices as will comfortably fit into the same pan and fry for a minute or so on each side. Remove to a warm platter. Arrange the quail's eggs on top of the slices and drizzle a little of the oil from the pan around them. Serve immediately.

**serves 4–6**
extra virgin olive oil, for cooking
16 quail's eggs
4 *sujuk* sausages, sliced on the diagonal

# mini lamb sausages

—— *maqaneq*

*Maqaneq* are tiny lamb sausages, highly seasoned with typical Lebanese spices, such as allspice, cinnamon, coriander, nutmeg and cloves, but they're not spicy hot. Try serving them with fried quail's eggs (as above).

Place a large non-stick frying pan over a medium-high heat. When hot, add the sausages and cook for 2–3 minutes, shaking the pan every now and then to ensure even cooking. Don't overcook them or they will harden. If you like, squeeze a little lemon juice over the sausages just before transferring them to a serving bowl to give them a little zing. Serve immediately.

**serves 4–6**
500g *maqaneq*
squeeze of lemon juice (optional)

# suppliers

The sources listed below are mostly in London as this is where I live and shop. However, this is not to say that you need to come to London to find specialist ingredients. In fact, because of the increasing popularity of Turkish, Greek, Lebanese and Moroccan food, many specialist ingredients are now found on supermarket shelves. For those less common ingredients, my advice is to ask the owner or chef at your nearest Middle Eastern restaurant – more and more are opening outside the capital – if they can recommend a local shop where you can find good specialist ingredients. I am sure that they will be more than happy to share their sources with you.

## Lebanese foods

Zen
27 Moscow Road
London W2
Tel: 020 7792 2058

Green Valley
37 Upper Berkeley Street
London W1H 5QE
Tel: 020 7402 7385

Maroush Deli
45–49 Edgware Road
London W2 2HZ
Tel: 0207 723 3666

Lebanese Food Centre
153–155 The Vale
London W3 7RX
Tel: 020 8740 7365

Damas Gate
81–85 Uxbridge Road
London W12 8NR
Tel: 0208 743 5116

## Turkish foods

Turkish Food Centre
589–591 Green Lanes
London N8 0RG
Tel: 020 8347 9950

Turkish Food Centre
89 Ridley Road
London E8 2NH
Tel: 020 7254 6754

## Moroccan foods

La Boucherie d'Or
105–107 Church Street
London, NW8 8EU
Tel: 020 7723 4573

Le Marrakech
64 Goldborne Road
London W10 5PS
Tel: 020 8964 8307

## General

The Spice Shop
1 Blenheim Crescent
London W11 2EE
Tel: 0207 221 4448
www.thespiceshop.co.uk

Maumoniat International
Food Supermarket
205 Dewsbury Road
Leeds
West Yorkshire LS11 5HT
Tel: 0113 200 8160

# index

# bibliography

Algar, Ayla *Classic Turkish Cooking*;
pub. HarperCollins, 1991, US

Davidson, Alan *The Oxford
Companion to Food*; pub. Oxford
University Press, 1999, UK

Guinaudeau, Franc Zette *Les Secrets
des Cusines en Terre Marocaine*;
pub. J P Taillendier, 1981, France

Halici, Nevin *Turkish Cookbook*;
pub. Dorling Kindersley, 1989, UK

Helou, Anissa *Lebanese Cuisine*;
pub. Grub Street, 2003, UK

Helou, Anissa *Street Café Morocco*;
pub. Conran Octopus, 1999, UK

Helou, Anissa *Mediterranean Street.
Food*; pub. Morrow, 2005, US

Kremezi, Aglaia *The Foods of Greece*;
pub. Stewart, Tabori & Chang,
1999, US

Mouzannar, Ibrahim *La Cuisine
Libanaise*; pub. Librairie du Liban,
1983, Lebanon

Norman, Jill *Herbs & Spices*;
pub. Dorling Kindersley, 2002, UK

Salaman, Rena *Greek Food*;
pub. HarperCollins, 1993. UK

This book is dedicated to Suni

## acknowledgements

First I would like to thank Elfreda Pownell without whom this book might not have come into being. Elfreda introduced me to Alison Cathie, my wonderful and supremely elegant publisher who, together with Jane O'Shea, equally wonderful and stylish, commissioned me to write this book.

Jane and Helen Lewis put together a perfect team to produce the book: Janet Illsley who edited my manuscript brilliantly; Claire Peters who designed the book beautifully; and Vanessa Courtier who took great photographs, graciously putting up with my fastidiousness in my kitchen. My thanks also to Clare Lattin for her terrific help with publicity.

I would also like to thank Susan Friedland for coming up with the title; Aglaia Kremezi for advice on all things Greek; Charles Perry for help with the transliteration; Peter Fuhrman for allowing me to use his house and kitchen to test recipes; Tracy West for testing recipes; Roberto Santibanez for advice on Mexican peppers; Mario, Michael, Ramiz and Ahmed at Zen Butchers; Mohamed Badralden and Ayman at Alwaha restaurant; John Blagden and everyone at Chalmers & Gray fishmongers; and Sally Clarke and all at & Clarke's.

My thanks also to my mother, Laurice Helou, who was always ready with advice on Lebanese mezze dishes and traditions; Nevin Halici, for letting me adapt her recipes, also Rena Salaman; Nayla Audi for letting me use her kibbé recipe; David Black, my American agent, and Susan Raihoffer, for introducing me to Caspian Dennis at Abner Stein who represents me here. And finally, apologies to those who have helped me and whom I have forgotten to mention.

**publishing director** Jane O'Shea
**creative director** Helen Lewis
**project editor** Janet Illsley
**designer** Claire Peters
**photographer** Vanessa Courtier
**food styling** Anissa Helou
**props styling** Wei Tang
**production** Ruth Deary

First published in 2007 by
Quadrille Publishing Limited,
Alhambra House, 27-31 Charing Cross Road
London WC2H 0LS
www.quadrille.co.uk

Text © 2007 Anissa Helou
Photography © 2007 Vanessa Courtier
Design and layout © 2007 Quadrille Publishing Limited

Cataloguing in Publication Data: a catalogue record for this book is available from the British Library.

ISBN 978 184400 461 4

Printed in Singapore